A
Treatise
on
Markets

A
Treatise
on
Markets
Spot, Futures, and Options

Joseph M. Burns

American Enterprise Institute for Public Policy Research
Washington, D.C.

Joseph M. Burns is a newly appointed member of the senior staff, Antitrust Division, U.S. Department of Justice. The study was completed during the author's service at the Commodity Futures Trading Commission.

Library of Congress Cataloging in Publication Data

Burns, Joseph M
    A treatise on markets.

    (Studies in economic policy)   (AEI studies ; 237)
      1. Commodity exchanges. 2. Put and call
transactions. I. Title. II. Series.
III. Series: American Enterprise Institute
for Public Policy Research. AEI studies ; 237.
HG6046.B87   332.6'44   79-14015
ISBN 0-8447-3340-7

AEI Studies 237

Printed in the United States of America

The development of the organism, whether social or physical, involves an increasing subdivision of functions between its separate parts on the one hand, and on the other a more intimate connection between them.

Alfred Marshall, *Principles of Economics*

CONTENTS

PREFACE

The development of markets is perhaps the most important aspect of the development of our free enterprise economy. And yet, economic analysts have devoted little attention to this subject. This neglect is both surprising and regrettable.

This study seeks to enhance understanding of the nature of spot markets, futures markets, and option markets. In particular, it is concerned with factors underlying the development of these markets and with the effects of market development on the economy. In this way, the study seeks to achieve its ultimate purpose—fostering a more meaningful basis for the consideration of economic policy.

The study began as an examination of the economic benefits of futures markets. In pursuing this objective, it quickly became evident that a full understanding of these benefits requires an understanding of how and why these markets exist.

Futures markets develop in response to forces—both demand and supply—in spot markets. More precisely, futures markets emerge from efficient spot markets. Recognition of this fact led me to examine the nature of efficient markets and also to analyze how and why spot markets become more efficient. In turn, the examination of spot markets provided useful insights for the analysis of futures markets. In addition, it pointed to the effects of both spot and futures markets on the development of option markets and to the repercussive effects of options on both spot and futures markets.

The Commodity Futures Trading Commission generously allowed me the time to pursue this inquiry in the manifold directions that my research appeared to require. All members of the commission, despite their time-consuming schedules and burdensome responsibilities, provided me every opportunity to discuss various issues with them. I particularly wish to thank Acting Chairman Gary Seevers.

During the course of this study, I have benefited from the constructive advice and criticism of my father, Arthur F. Burns, as well as from Milton Friedman, Phillip Cagan, and Thomas Johnson. I have also benefited from discussions on special points with Moses Abramovitz, Roger Grey, Ronald Hobson, Henry Jarecki, Marvin Kosters, and Charles Siegman. I owe a debt of gratitude to several members of the commission staff—particularly Melissa Reese—for their efficient handling of my manuscript. No acknowledgment here would be complete without some mention of my intellectual indebtedness to my former teacher and thesis adviser, the late Harry G. Johnson.

A draft of this study was submitted to the Commodity Futures Trading Commission in September 1978, and was then circulated among interested scholars. This study is a revised version of that draft.

The views expressed herein are solely those of the author and are not intended to reflect those of the Commission or other members of the staff.

JOSEPH M. BURNS
Washington, D.C.
February 1979

1
Introduction

To some people, futures and option markets are incomprehensible. To others, they are iniquitous—causing high prices to consumers, low prices to producers, and excessive fluctuations of prices, as well as providing a forum for speculators or gamblers. These views are attributable, in part at least, to a lack of understanding of the economic role of futures and option markets and of speculators' contribution to that role.

This study seeks to provide a foundation for understanding how futures and option markets serve the public interest—that is, the interests of the national and international economies. To do this, it analyzes the raison d'être, nature, and economic benefits of these markets. On the basis of this analysis, the study explores the economic rationale for the regulation of these markets.

Futures markets typically develop in response to economic forces—supply as well as demand—in spot markets. In turn, futures markets facilitate the working of spot markets. This study therefore analyzes markets in general, with special attention to spot markets, prior to the analysis of futures markets.

The study then turns to the analysis of option markets. Option markets typically develop in response to supply and demand forces in spot and/or futures markets and, in turn, help spot and futures markets to work better.

The analysis of markets in general, with special attention to spot markets, provides a useful framework for understanding futures markets. In particular, the principles developed in the analysis of spot markets apply also to futures markets. The study also examines the forces in spot markets that prompt, as well as facilitate, the development of futures markets. In a similar way, the analysis of

1

spot and futures markets provides a useful framework for understanding option markets.

This study shows that futures and option markets, like other financial markets, are molded by forces in the real (as distinct from the financial) sector of the economy and that all financial markets, in turn, affect the real sector. The more developed financial markets, such as futures and option markets, may be molded directly by financial as well as by real forces. In turn, the more developed financial markets may directly affect financial and real markets.

The study also explores factors conducive to a market's development and the economic effects of its development. The factors prompting a market's development and the effects of its development are inherently interrelated. Indeed, understanding why a market develops helps to explain its economic benefits.

As an economy and its markets develop, markets become increasingly specialized: from rudimentary local spot markets to centralized spot markets, to forward markets, to futures markets and decentralized spot markets, and to option markets for futures and actuals (the assets traded on spot markets). The study shows that the specialization of markets is accompanied by increasingly close market interrelationships involving the efficiency of markets as well as the prices generated in them.

In view of the interrelationship of markets in an advanced free enterprise economy, a well-functioning market may provide immense benefits to the real sector of the economy. Because the various markets are interrelated, however, any malfunctioning in one market may have pervasive deleterious effects. For this reason, the orderly functioning of markets—particularly the more developed ones—is important to the economy.

The principal economic purpose of market regulation—whether of spot, futures, or option markets—has been to promote their orderly functioning. This objective requires mitigating, if not preventing, disorderly market conditions and enhancing the quality of market organization. This study will explore the meaning of these concepts and their implications for governmental regulation.

The next chapter analyzes the nature and development of markets, with special attention to spot markets. Chapters 3 and 4 analyze similar aspects of futures and option markets, respectively. Chapter 5 examines the economic benefits of market development. Chapter 6 discusses the regulation of markets, with special attention to futures and options. And Chapter 7 offers some concluding observations, including a discussion of the paradox associated with futures and option markets—namely, the widespread criticism of these markets that exists in the face of their substantial public benefits.

2
Spot Markets

Some Prefatory Comments

A market is a mechanism for effecting purchases and sales of assets and services in a relatively public manner. Thus, a market entails a way of carrying out transactions and some means of collecting and disseminating information on the terms of transactions, particularly price. These two aspects of a market are inherently interrelated.

The economic demand for effecting transactions precedes the economic demand for information (especially price information). This precedence is more a matter of logic than of actual sequence, inasmuch as the demand for effecting transactions immediately gives rise to the demand for information concerning the terms of a transaction. The logical connection emphasizes an important point: the means of collecting and disseminating information are designed to facilitate the carrying out of transactions.

For any asset, the ways of carrying out transactions are a product of commercial needs and practices, which in turn reflect real demand and supply capabilities. The ways of effecting transactions give rise to, and are molded by, methods of collecting and disseminating information on the terms of transactions. The collection and dissemination of information on the terms of transactions have become increasingly specialized in line with increasing specialization in carrying out of transactions.

Over time, practically all aspects of transactions have become standardized, leaving little other than price to vary. This simplifies the collection and dissemination of price information. All price information mechanisms, however, have an inherent problem: a price quotation for a commodity, security, or any other type of asset can be strictly accurate only at a particular location or locations, at a particular instant of time, and for a particular quality, size, and type of transaction. The quality of information mechanisms differs among assets as well as for a given asset over time.

For a system of price information to be economically feasible, the practices for effecting transactions must be at least fairly well developed. In turn, introducing or improving a system of providing information facilitates the carrying out of transactions.

It is useful to make two types of distinction among markets: by type of asset or service and by time for completing transactions. Markets may relate to real assets (such as land, capital, and commodities) or to financial assets (such as bonds, common stock, and commercial paper). This distinction is based on the nature of the asset (or service) that is traded. A physical asset and a financial asset often differ in another respect: a security is issued by a specific private or public entity, whereas a commodity may or may not be unique to a particular producer. The commodities that lend themselves to market development usually are not unique products of a particular enterprise.

Financial markets came into existence after the emergence of real markets. It is often difficult to distinguish early financial assets and markets from real ones, however. Real assets and markets gradually became more and more specialized, and this process at times culminated in the birth of financial assets and markets. For example, the earliest loans consisted of an exchange of present physical goods for future physical goods. Such a market would be considered real in nature. When and where physical assets took on the functions of money, however, the market became a financial one. Historically, the introduction of money was a response to market forces— namely, the increasing cost of barter as a method of effecting increasingly diverse and complex transactions. The evolution of money was a gradual process, however, and for a period of time there was no clear dividing line between real and financial assets or markets.

Markets may relate either to spot or to future transactions. This distinction is based on the time at which transactions are to be completed. In some markets—spot markets—transactions are completed immediately; in others, transactions agreed to at one point in time are consummated at some stated future time.

Markets (real or financial) do not exist in a vacuum. They develop in response to persistent needs and economic demands for more efficient mechanisms to carry out transactions and to collect and disseminate information on the terms of these transactions. The development of a market may refer to establishing a new market or to enhancing the "efficiency" or expanding the size of an already existing one. The efficiency of a market is an important concept in the analysis of market development and in the assessment of the attendant economic benefits.

The Meaning of Market Efficiency

The efficiency of a market is a function of its liquidity, the orderliness of market conditions, and the quality of a market's organization. Each of these aspects is important, and yet none of them has received sufficient attention. In part, this may reflect excessive concentration on the analysis of stationary markets—such as perfect competition, monopolistic competition, or pure monopoly—in which development in regard to market efficiency is by definition subsumed away. In the stationary concept, "efficient markets" are those "in which prices always 'fully reflect' available information."[1] This definition diverts attention from the fact that efficiency of a market is a variable to be explained rather than a constant exogenously given. A broader concept of market efficiency is a necessary basis for understanding how and why markets develop and what effects their development has on the economy.

The liquidity of a market is the principal element of a market's efficiency. Liquidity fosters orderly market conditions and influences the character of a market's organization. In turn, orderly market conditions and good market organization promote market liquidity.

The orderliness of market conditions and quality of a market's

---

[1] This definition appears in Eugene Fama, "Efficient Capital Markets: A Review of Theory and Empirical Evidence," *Journal of Finance*, vol. 25, no. 2 (May 1970), pp. 383-417, emphasis in original. The roots of this definition appear to lie—unfortunately but not surprisingly—in the fact that empirical work on market efficiency preceded the development of theory in this area. In this connection, Fama observed, "Though we proceed from theory to empirical evidence, to keep the proper historical perspective we should note that to a large extent the empirical work in this area preceded the development of the theory." The technological advances in computerization may be in part responsible for the precedence of empirical work to theoretical work in this area (as well as in many others).

The conventional use of the concept "market efficiency" does recognize three forms of efficiency. William Beaver, for example, distinguished between "The weak form, which deals with efficiency—with respect to the past sequence of security prices (for example, the random-walk hypothesis), (2) the semi-strong form, which concerns efficiency with respect to published information, and (3) the strong form, which involves all information including inside information." William Beaver, "What Should Be the FASB's Objectives?" *Journal of Accountancy*, vol. 136, no. 2 (August 1973), pp. 49-56.

organization are also closely related. They are the crux of a market's orderly functioning (or operating efficiency). A market's functioning is orderly—in a given economic environment, including prevailing policies of government—to the degree that the optimal benefits of that market are in existence.[2] Market regulation is generally directed towards enhancing the orderly functioning of markets. Unless the full benefits of the orderly functioning of markets are understood, regulation may be carried too far or not far enough. Indeed, it is important that the perceived and actual usefulness of regulation be the same.

Liquidity of a Market. Market liquidity, or liquidity of an asset traded on a market, has two aspects: certainty of price (liquidity proper), and expected marketability.[3] Liquidity proper refers to the degree of certainty, or predictability, of an asset's underlying value. An asset's underlying value refers to an asset's value if no time constraints were imposed on its disposal and if conditions in the market remained constant.[4] Thus, liquidity proper depends on how much is known about an asset's underlying value. Assets, such as securities, that are traded on organized exchanges are high in liquidity proper compared to assets, such as used cars, that are traded on highly segmented markets.

The expected marketability of an asset refers to the expected ease or difficulty of approximately realizing the asset's underlying value during the period of time allowed for its disposal. Expected marketability is a function of the expected bid-asked price spread, expected brokerage costs, and the uncertainty attached to these expectations.

With a constant demand schedule, a larger volume of a given asset is, by definition, less marketable than a smaller volume—that is, the larger the volume of a given asset put up for sale, the lower will be the price, and thus the further away from its underlying value. However, there may be economies of scale involved in a transaction (such as for hundred-share blocks of a given security) that make this relationship operational only after a certain volume of an asset has been traded.

---

[2] The term "optimal benefits" is defined as full potential benefits net of the costs of securing them.

[3] See Joseph M. Burns, "On the Effects of Financial Innovations," *Quarterly Review of Economics and Business*, vol. 11, no. 2 (Summer 1971), pp. 83-95, esp. pp. 87-88.

[4] Because market conditions do not remain constant, most assets' underlying value (at any given point in time) can never be known with certainty.

Marketability is a multidimensional concept. In particular, the more time allowed for the disposal of an asset, the higher its expected net sale price.[5] Thus, at a given point in time, an asset is likely to have different degrees of marketability depending on how much time is allowed for its disposition. It is not impossible that one asset, which is more marketable than another in a short disposal period, might be less marketable in a long disposal period.

The two aspects of liquidity—certainty of price and expected marketability—are closely related. The more certain an asset's underlying value is expected to be, the greater should be its marketability. Indeed, the ease of realizing an asset's approximate underlying value is directly related to the certainty of that value. The converse—the more marketable an asset, the greater the degree of certainty of its underlying value—is also true, *ceteris paribus*.

All markets are—to some degree—illiquid, or incomplete, in their development. Uncertainty and transaction costs are facts of life. They can be mitigated in one way or another, but they cannot be eliminated.

An asset's liquidity often is confused with the volume of trading in that asset.[6] It is true that a liquid market fosters trading, but it is entirely possible that no transactions will occur in a liquid asset over a period of time—with or without a change of bid-asked price quotations. For example, even if no transactions took place on a given day in IBM stock, the price of the stock would be well known and might even change based on a change in bid-asked price quotations. This situation could arise under conditions of reasonably similar expectations—specific to the asset as well as in general—by all holders (actual and potential) of the asset. Another condition favoring such a situation is reasonably constant attitudes towards risk by all holders of the asset. Because these conditions are seldom met, however, there is usually a large volume of transactions in a liquid asset.

Orderliness of Market Conditions. "Orderly market conditions" (or disorderly ones) is an important concept for government regulatory agencies. However, the term is seldom defined with any precision.[7]

---

[5] An optimal amount of transaction cost is assumed to be incurred so as to realize the maximum expected net price during the period of time considered.

[6] See, for example, the proceedings of the North Central Regional Conference on Pricing Problems in the Food Industry (with Emphasis on Thin Markets), Commodity Futures Trading Commission, Washington, D.C., March 2, 1978.

[7] See, for example, quarterly foreign exchange reports of the Federal Reserve Bank of New York during the 1970s. On one occasion, in response to a question at a congressional hearing, the chairman of the Board of Governors of

The term, "disorderly market conditions," often is used to refer to movements in prices, such as sharp increases or decreases and high volatility.[8] "Disorderly market conditions" is also used to refer to increases in bid-asked price spreads, as well as (at times) to attendant declines in the volume of trading.[9] Both types of usage may be inappropriate and misleading. Indeed, such price movements, as well as changes in price spreads and volume of trading, may well constitute an efficient response of a market to new information or to a changed appraisal of existing information (including a change in confidence attached to the appraisals). Both usages do appear to characterize the symptoms of some disorderly market conditions, but an understanding of "disorderly market conditions" requires knowledge of the sources of such symptoms or problems.

"Disorderly" refers to a situation in which a market is not operating properly within a given economic environment. Under such circumstances, the optimal benefits of the market cannot be realized. At least three types of disorderly market conditions may be usefully distinguished:

1. A disorderly condition may exist when the price of a transaction is off a market's demand and/or supply schedules. Artificial barriers to market entry—through monopolies or monopsonies—are examples of such a condition.

2. In certain circumstances, a market may be susceptible to manipulation, not because of artificial barriers to market entry, but rather because of artificial barriers to market information that allow false rumors to circulate. If such rumors mislead a market's participants, they will generate a price that is temporarily artificial and misleading. The existence of private monopolies or governmental vacillation on some policy matter, together with a lack of public information on the parameters affecting the outcome, foster this type of disorderly market condition.

the Federal Reserve System, did seek to define "disorderly markets" with some precision. See Federal Reserve Board staff memorandum on disorderly markets in U.S. Congress, Joint Economic Committee, *The 1973 Midyear Review of the Economy*, 93rd Congress, 1st session, p. 240.

[8] There is an interesting asymmetry in the use of the term, "disorderly market conditions." With regard to interest rates, "disorderly market conditions" typically has been used in the context of rising interest rates (especially before 1951), not falling interest rates. With regard to exchange rates, this term typically has been used in the context of declining values of the dollar (especially in the 1970s), not rising values.

[9] Usually, the bid-asked spreads that are referred to (implicitly or explicitly), as well as those that are in fact examined, are marginal spreads. What is important, however, is the entire structure of bid-asked price quotations and changes therein.

Some rumors may be governmental trial balloons—an attempt to gauge the response to a policy option. To the extent that such rumors suggest a more definitive policy position than in fact exists, they are misleading and may affect the market adversely, especially in the long run. Not all rumors are deliberately false in nature, however. Many rumors are the products of thoughtful conjecture and/or inadvertent leaks by a governmental source. Such rumors, even if they eventually turn out to be inaccurate, may help the market by providing new or better information.[10]

3. A wide price swing occasioned by overreaction to a prior price trend may also create a disorderly market. This condition often has been characterized as destabilizing speculation. Such price behavior, however, could be brought about by any type of trader—commercial firm or speculator—in the market. It spells inefficiencies in markets only to the extent that such price behavior is traceable to artificial factors.

Such wide price swings often are thought to produce a disorderly market if the price is moving in a direction opposite to that ultimately expected by the traders. In this case, traders avoid taking a position in the market that they otherwise would take and wait until the trend has run its course before taking a position.[11] This situation results in inefficiency only when there are artificial barriers to market use, such as restrictions on short positions or limitations on speculative positions. Under these constraints, traders are not always able to take full advantage of their judgment about the market's prospective behavior. As a result, price would not always reflect the full

---

[10] It is possible that rumor-induced price movements—even if deliberately false or misleading—will have some desirable side effects. They may, for example, lead to wider recognition of problems inherent in government inaction or ambiguity. To the extent that rumor-induced price movements make the government more aware of its deficiencies, they indirectly generate some benefits (as well as costs). In all probability, however, rumor-induced price movements will not have frequent or substantial beneficial effects, owing to the nature of governmental decision making in a democratic society such as ours.

[11] Cf. John Maynard Keynes, *The General Theory of Employment, Interest, and Money* (New York: Harcourt, Brace, and Co., 1958), ch. 12. It should be recognized, however, that those making trades on the basis of so-called trends often (if not usually) lose money. Trends are easier to ascertain ex post than ex ante. Empirical research on prices in various markets does not support the existence of profit opportunities on the basis of charts and technical rules. Indeed, as B. A. Goss and B. S. Yamey point out, "The findings of the various empirical studies can be summarized to the effect that there is little evidence in support of price dependence. Price series exhibit the characteristics of a random walk in that the increments or decrements linking successive prices tend to be randomly distributed." "Introduction: The Economics of Futures Trading" in B. A. Goss and B. S. Yamey, eds., *The Economics of Futures Trading* (New York: Halstead Press, 1976). Also, cf. Fama, "Efficient Capital Markets."

forces of supply and demand. The artificial factor may slow the adjustment of price to market forces and thereby contribute to wider swings in prices over the long run than would otherwise occur.

Quality of Market Organization. A market may or may not be organized. The organization of a market embraces the institutions that directly service a market—the brokers, exchanges, and (at times) clearinghouses and inspection services. The quality of a market's organization refers to the operating efficiency of such institutions. The operating efficiency of the institutions should be considered in the context of the market's liquidity. Indeed, the more liquid a market, the more developed the market's organization typically is.

Highly liquid markets, such as organized security markets, typically have an intricate and specialized system for effecting transactions and for collecting and disseminating relevant information. In such markets, virtually all aspects of transactions are specified, except for level of price. Precise specification of the nonprice terms of transactions simplifies the collection and dissemination of information on actual prices.

Factors Conducive to Market Efficiency

Certain factors contribute to the presence of the three interrelated aspects of market efficiency. The primary focus here is on private forces that affect the efficiency of a market.

The absence of many types of markets and the low level of efficiency of others should not be viewed as a deficiency of the free enterprise system. Private forces determine both the types of markets that do emerge and the level of their efficiency. The interrelationship of market development (real and financial) and private forces in the real sector is important, but it has not been sufficiently explored.[12] One possible reason is that economists do not ask often enough the question, "Why do things happen in certain cases and not in others?" A second possible reason is that economists usually lack the second-by-second knowledge of the market that often is crucial to a full understanding of why things happen in certain cases and not in others.

---

[12] See, however, Frederick Lavington, *The English Capital Market* (London: Methuen and Co., Ltd., 1921); John G. Gurley and E. S. Shaw, *Money in a Theory of Finance* (Washington: The Brookings Institution, 1960); and Joseph Burns, "The Saving-Investment Process in a Theory of Finance" (unpublished Ph.D. dissertation, University of Chicago, 1967).

Market Liquidity. A number of factors affect the liquidity of an asset traded on a market. The breadth and urgency of demand, the cost of ascertaining an asset's quality, the expected cost of default, the cost of transporting an asset, and the cost of holding inventories are proximate determinants of the emergence of a market (positive liquidity) and the degree of liquidity of existing markets.[13] These factors are interrelated, and each is a function of numerous other factors. The factors responsible for a market's liquidity vary from one market to another and also vary over time for a given market.

Breadth and urgency of demand. The degree of universality and urgency of demand are basic to a market's liquidity. Indeed, for a market to exist, there must be the expectation of strong and reasonably persistent demand generated by numerous entities. Stated differently, the prospective volume of trading, and the value per trade, must be sufficient to justify starting a market. The liquidity of already existing markets is enhanced by an increase in the number of entities desiring a particular asset as well as by an increase in the economic demands of present users.

This factor—the breadth and urgency of demand—helps to explain the early development of spot markets for agricultural products. It also helps to explain the development of spot markets for industrial raw materials in the eighteenth and nineteenth centuries and the rapid development of foreign exchange markets for the increasingly interdependent national economies of the twentieth century.

Cost of ascertaining an asset's quality. A low cost of ascertaining an asset's quality encourages transactions in the asset.[14] In such situations, transaction costs may be nominal, amounting to little more than transfer costs, because search costs to determine the quality of an asset will be small. With little effort needed for intensive search of an asset's quality, effort may be devoted almost entirely to extensive search for the best purchase or sale price of an asset. Extensive price search is conducive to a high degree of marketability, and—more broadly—to a high degree of liquidity.

---

[13] Cf. Alfred Marshall, *Principles of Economics*, Ninth Edition (New York: Macmillan Co., 1961), vol. 1, bk. 5, ch. 1.

[14] A low cost of ascertaining an asset's quantity also facilitates the carrying out of transactions. Historically, ascertaining an asset's quantity has been much less of a problem than ascertaining its quality; the quantification of most assets by number, weight, or measure has been reasonably easy—at least, after the primitive stages of economic development.

Several factors may lower the cost of obtaining information about the quality of an asset. They relate to the nature of the asset, the nature of the producer, and the quality of overall market information.

1. Information can be readily obtained about the quality of real assets, such as commodities, that are homogeneous in nature or that can easily be standardized through grading. Usually, the cost of ascertaining the quality of such assets is low, and their markets are relatively liquid.

The degree of homogeneity and the cost of standardization differ enormously among assets, which helps to explain why some markets have become liquid and others have not. For example, it helps to explain the development of liquid spot markets for commodities, such as wheat, corn, and cotton, and the absence of such markets for real estate. In addition, it helps to explain why there are liquid spot markets for commodities at an early stage of production—at or near the raw condition—but not for the same commodities at a later stage of production (processing).

Standardization may be viewed as an information-producing activity that makes it easier to ascertain the quality of assets. Establishing or improving standardization of an asset encourages liquid markets to develop and thereby increases demand for such assets. A large volume of trade of an impersonal character fosters standardization; in this situation, standardization can generate substantial benefits through economies of scale.

Grading of commodities is a method of standardizing quality. For the grains, grading has become quite developed; grades are based on a number of factors, including moisture content and purity of type. Grading should be sufficiently flexible to adapt to changes in technology.

Grading was initially done entirely by the private sector. However done, grading entails a cost. This service will be provided by the private sector if producers, consumers, and dealers are willing to pay for it. Dealers and exchanges frequently promote the practice of quality specification in order to augment the volume of trade. Thus, standardization of quality was both a natural byproduct of, and a contributor to, the expansion of trade.

2. Information can be readily obtained about the quality of financial assets, such as corporate securities, that are issued by well-known firms. Usually, the cost of ascertaining the quality of such assets is low, and this fosters the development of liquid markets for them.

Confidence in the issuer was important in the development of liquid spot markets for securities of blue-chip companies and stable governments, and the lack of such confidence helps to explain the absence of liquid markets for securities of relatively unknown firms and of countries whose governments are regarded as unstable.

In the same vein, assets with a low degree of risk are likely to be more liquid than assets whose future prices are less certain. This difference in liquidity may be attributable to a difference in the ease of obtaining information about the asset. In turn, differences in liquidity augment existing differences in risk.

In contrast to liquidity in commodity markets, which generally is greater for commodities in an early stage of production, liquidity in securities markets usually is greater for securities of firms whose products are individualized. Indeed, a company that invests resources in establishing recognition of its name (GM or IBM) or its product's brand name (Xerox, Kleenex, Pepsi Cola) may be able to increase the liquidity of its securities.

Establishing a reputation is an information-producing activity that makes it easier to ascertain the quality of a security. Brand-name investments foster the demand for an asset—directly as well as indirectly—by enhancing its liquidity. The large volume and the impersonal character of trade induce investments in name recognition; pronounced profits from such investments are then realizable through economies of scale.

Investments designed to foster a company's name recognition may be among the most important that a company undertakes. Indeed, once most companies have experienced reasonably consistent and profitable returns, they devote large amounts of resources to this activity. A company's (or government's) reputation is, however, more difficult to change for the better than for the worse. Once a reputation deteriorates—which may happen very quickly—it may take years to restore it. The effects of Watergate and related events on the perceived integrity of the U.S. government may well be with us for a long time.

The incorporation of a business does more than reduce the risk hazards of its owners; it tends to enhance market information about the firm.

Financial rating services, such as Moody's and Standard and Poor's, produce market information by evaluating individual securities. For such services to be established, a pool of differentiated securities must already be in existence; in this situation, pronounced benefits (profits of these services) are then realizable through economies of scale.

Financial intermediation, such as that provided by savings and loan associations or mutual funds, is also an application of economies of scale to the production of information about asset quality. Indeed, financial intermediation may be viewed as a device for transforming risk-prone, illiquid assets of individual entities into safe, liquid assets by pooling risk (both of customers' withdrawal of funds and of default on assets purchased) and by applying the intermediary's own brand name to the assets.[15] The securities (including deposits) issued by financial intermediaries are typically quite safe and liquid compared to most of the assets these institutions purchase.

3. Improvements in information about markets or market sectors make it easier to judge the quality of an asset. This decreases uncertainty about the asset's underlying value and increases its marketability, thereby enhancing liquidity.

Improvements in information may take many forms and arise in different ways. An increase in the volume and complexity of trade generates an increased demand for market information. As a result, improvements may be induced in the provision of market information; larger benefits (profits) from improvements in information services, such as market news reports, are then realizable through economies of scale. These improvements enhance market liquidity. They also tend to induce improvements in communication; it is now easier to collect and disseminate information about market conditions. With improvements in communication, prices are reported more accurately and comprehensively, and the reports are distributed faster and with greater clarity. As a result, price differences for similar transactions are narrowed; the introduction of the transatlantic cable and the telegraph system, for example, had this effect.[16] Such improvements also are likely to reduce bid-asked spreads and the premiums and discounts for quality differentials. In general, improvements in communication reduce uncertainty about market prices, thereby fostering market liquidity.

Better information about demand-supply conditions surrounding a specific asset may come from many sources—new exchanges or dealers, for example. These sources may also provide better information about related assets—substitutes, complements, the same

---

[15] See Burns, "On the Effects of Financial Innovations."
[16] Kenneth D. Garbade and William L. Silber, "Technology, Communication and the Performance of Financial Markets: 1840-1975," *Journal of Finance*, vol. 33, no. 3 (June 1978).

assets in other geographical locations, or the same asset at other points in time.

The liquidity of a particular spot market is affected not only by information bearing directly on that market but also by many other kinds of information—particularly, information about the future price of the asset. The better the information about an asset's expected future spot price, the greater its current liquidity will be, *ceteris paribus*. Thus, the development of markets for future transactions, which improves information about an asset's expected future spot price, enhances the liquidity of spot markets.

Expected cost of default. The expected cost of default depends on default risk (the expected probability of default and the uncertainty attached to these expectations), together with the cost of enforcement for a given default (the expected cost of enforcement and the uncertainty attached to these expectations). A low expected cost of default promotes the marketability of an asset and thus fosters market liquidity.

Virtually all contracts are burdened by some expected cost of default inasmuch as some default risk attends virtually all contracts. This risk may be either involuntary (that an entity will be unable, because of financial considerations, to abide by its agreement) and/or voluntary (that an entity will be unwilling, because of moral turpitude, to abide by its agreement). In addition, few contracts are completely enforceable. On this latter point, Kenneth Arrow has stated:

> there is no way to insure complete enforceability. An individual may make a contract which he cannot in fact fulfill. Penalties may indeed be imposed on failure to live up to one's agreement, but they are not a substitute for compliance from the viewpoint of the other party, and there is always a degree of cost in enforcing the penalties. The laws of bankruptcy are a social recognition that complete enforceability is impossible and that it is even socially desirable to set limits on the penalties for failure.[17]

The two aspects of expected cost of default—default risk and enforcement costs—are related. In particular, the moral (voluntary) risk of default usually is larger for contracts whose enforcement is difficult than for those that are easy to enforce. Stated differently,

---

[17] Kenneth Arrow, "Limited Knowledge and Economic Analysis," *American Economic Review*, vol. 64, no. 1 (March 1974), p. 8.

fraud does not happen capriciously; rather, it tends to occur in situations in which contractual enforcement is difficult.

Moral risk differs among countries, independently of enforcement costs. These differences may be related to differences in the magnitude and extent of religious training and convictions. Moral risk also exists in dealings between countries—in the form of political risk—and here, too, differences exist. Democratic governments appear to foster low political risk, perhaps because the conscience of the people as opposed to a person is a better guarantee of responsible governmental behavior.

Default risk—both voluntary and involuntary—can be reduced by insurance. Involuntary default, however, is easier to insure than moral risk, because of the availability of more actuarial information. Political risk, a special case of moral risk, is one of the most difficult to insure: first, the risks entailed are not likely to be independent; second, past experience is not likely to be adequate in providing precise actuarial tables on possible default. Although commercial insurance can deal with this type of risk, its cost is prohibitive in most cases.[18]

Enforcement costs vary among countries according to the countries' willingness and ability to define and enforce rights to the possession of property. The willingness to do this depends on national mores and traditions, and on the volume and complexity of property disputes; the ability to do this also depends on national mores and traditions as well as on the quality of the legal system and governmental law enforcement.

---

[18] The lack of independence in possible outcomes does not mean that probabilities of default cannot be calculated; rather, it means that the probability distribution will not be normal. The resulting greater covariation of possible defaults will mean that the expected variance of possible outcomes will be greater than that entailed in a normal distribution. For this reason, the risk will be greater and the requisite premium higher than would be entailed with a normal distribution.

The fact that past experience is not likely to be adequate in providing precise actuarial tables on possible default also does not mean that probabilities cannot be calculated; rather, it means that the prior probabilities are held with less confidence than that entailed with some other forms of risk. This lack of confidence will mean that the expected variance in possible outcomes will be still greater. As a result, the risk will be even greater and the requisite premium still higher.

These points are from Joseph M. Burns, "Alleged Market Failures in Financing U.S. Exports," U.S. Congress, House of Representatives, Subcommittee on International Security and Scientific Affairs of the Committee on International Relations, *Hearings on Nuclear Proliferation: Future Foreign Policy Implications*, 94th Congress, 1st session, pp. 386-88.

A large volume of trade, together with its impersonal character, encourages countries to develop a system of property rights. In turn, a system of property rights enhances market liquidity and thus increases the volume of trade and its impersonal character.

Growth in the volume and impersonalized nature of trade, of itself, could multiply default cost problems. However, trade expansion and the impersonalization of the marketplace could, as it did in this country, lead dealers to demand equitable as well as efficient trade practices. The development of trading rules on organized exchanges, including provision for contractual enforcement, was a response to this economic demand. The standardization of trade practices has made it easier to assess the risk of default, and the enforceability of contracts has reduced the costs associated with a given default.

The expected cost of default on forward contracts is higher than on spot transactions: first, the probability of default—both voluntary (moral) and especially involuntary—is greater and more uncertain; second, the difficulty (or cost) of enforcement, for a given default, is greater. On this issue, Kenneth Arrow has stated:

> when the exchange of values for values is simultaneous or nearly so, the contracts may almost be self-enforcing. If a good has been sold and not paid for, it can be recovered; if there is a continuing relation of buyer and seller, a failure to settle bills can be met by refusal to make further deliveries, in which case the loss is minimized. With contracts extending into the distant future, on the contrary, the possibility of failure to comply becomes greater, partly because the self-enforcement aspects become weaker, partly because unexpected changes may intervene to make even a sincerely intended compliance difficult or impossible.[19]

The higher expected cost of default on forward contracts than on spot transactions has delayed the introduction of forward markets and constrained their development.

Cost of transporting an asset. Another factor affecting the liquidity of an asset is the ease with which it can be carried, or transported, from place to place. The easier it is to transport an asset, the more marketable and thereby the more liquid it becomes.

The cost of transporting an asset from place to place depends on transportation technology. Low costs of transportation expand the breadth of an asset's market. Thus, low-cost transportation

---

[19] Arrow, "Limited Knowledge."

promotes integration of local markets into one or more central, or terminal, markets, with all the benefits that such integration brings. A central market (such as the Chicago grain market), is highly liquid. Its high liquidity stimulates its use, which further augments its liquidity. The prospective benefits of low transportation costs, in turn, induce technological improvements (such as packaging) designed to enhance the transportability of products.

Increasing contacts between economic communities usually bring about improvements in transportation. In turn, improvements in transportation induce improvements in the collection and dissemination of information. Because of the wider market for goods, the firms that supply market information have incentive to improve their services.

The ease, or cost, of transporting an asset between locations differs among assets. The cost of transporting assets whose value is high in relation to their bulk (gold and silver, for example) is usually low per dollar of value. This increases their liquidity.

Cost of holding inventories. The ease with which an asset can be held over time also affects its liquidity. The easier it is to carry, or hold, an asset over time, the more marketable and thereby the more liquid it becomes.

Low costs of carrying an asset over time encourage asset owners to hold inventories (actual or potential). The ability to hold inventories is useful, both to the asset's owner and to its market.

A commercial firm seeking to improve its profits may wish to hold inventories for three reasons. The first reason is to improve its ability to sell what its customers seek to buy; without inventories, sales and therefore also profits would probably be lower.

Second, inventories held for a relatively long period—say, three months rather than three days—enhance an asset's marketability (and liquidity). The extension of a market over time (actual or potential)—that is, the lengthening of the period for an asset's disposal—permits an increase of information about the asset in question, thereby enhancing the prospect that when sold its underlying value will be approximated. Firms lengthen the period (actual or potential) an asset is carried, because they expect the benefits from increased marketability to outweigh the expected costs of the longer carrying period.

Third, a "commercial" firm's holding of inventories (actual or potential) may also increase the return that it expects to realize, not only because of the asset's increased marketability but also because the asset's price (underlying value) may improve over time. This

20

reason for holding inventories—the expectation of a higher price—is analytically different from the preceding ones. Empirically, however, it would be difficult, if not impossible, to distinguish commercial and speculative inventory holdings: the benefits of each are based on uncertain expectations, hence each may generate some benefits of the other type.

The holding of inventory—whatever the purpose—was originally carried out by commercial firms (dealers as well as producers). Later, speculative investors outside the immediate trade acquired goods for storage in the hope of realizing higher prices (underlying values).[20] Both commercial firms and speculative investors earn a return from buying commodities and holding them off the market at times when supplies are abundant and prices are low, and placing them on the market later when relative scarcity raises the price.

To the extent that the speculative holding of inventories is (on balance) successful, it performs a useful economic function by reducing swings in commodity prices.[21] The smaller swings in

---

[20] The speculative investors in spot markets were the forerunners of the speculative investors, or so-called speculators, in futures and options.

[21] On this point, John Stuart Mill has stated: "This effect [the reduction of price fluctuations] is much promoted by the existence of large capitals, belonging to what are called speculative merchants, whose business it is to buy goods in order to resell them at a profit.

"These dealers naturally buying things when they are cheapest, and storing them up to be brought again into the market when the price has become unusually high; the tendency of their operations is to equalize price, or at least to moderate its inequalities. The prices of things are neither so much depressed at one time, nor so much raised at another, as they would be if speculative dealers did not exist.

"Speculators, therefore, have a highly useful office in the economy of society; and (contrary to common opinion) the most useful portion of the class are those who speculate in commodities affected by the vicissitudes of seasons. If there were no corn-dealers, not only would the price of corn be liable to variations much more extreme than at present, but in a deficient season the necessary supplies might not be forthcoming at all. Unless there were speculators in corn, or unless, in default of dealers, the farmers became speculators, the price in a season of abundance would fall without any limit or check, except the wasteful consumption that would invariably follow. That any part of the surplus of one year remains to supply the deficiency of another, is owing either to farmers who withhold corn from the market, or to dealers who buy it when at the cheapest and lay it up in store. . . .

"When a speculation in a commodity proves profitable to the speculators as a body, it is because, in the interval between their buying and reselling, the price rises from some cause independent of them, their only connection with it consisting in having foreseen it. In this case, their purchases make the price begin to rise sooner than it otherwise would do, thus spreading the privation of the consumers over a longer period, but mitigating it at the time of its greatest height: evidently to the general advantage . . . The operations, therefore, of speculative dealers, are useful to the public whenever profitable to them-

commodity prices foster expectations of greater long-run price stability. In turn, the reduction of price risk fosters an increase of commercial demand for inventories, and the resultant increase of inventory holdings enhances the liquidity of spot markets. In this way, the speculative demand for inventories directly promotes larger commercial demand. The expectations of more stable long-run prices also reduces the uncertainty facing commodity producers. This encourages production, which also tends to enhance market liquidity.

The speculative holding of inventories strengthens the liquidity of spot markets not only through its price-stabilizing effects but also by increasing the number of market participants.

The low cost of carrying securities is conducive to speculative investment in securities markets—in fact, it accounts for the greater volume of speculative investment in these markets than in commodity markets. The decreased price fluctuations that result from successful (on balance) speculation serve to enhance the prestige of a company, making its securities more liquid. Speculative investment in securities markets also directly enhances the liquidity of these markets.

---

selves; and though they are sometimes injurious to the public, by heightening the fluctuations which their more usual office is to alleviate, yet whenever this happens the speculators are the greatest losers. The interest, in short, of the speculators as a body, coincides with the interest of the public. . . ." John Stuart Mill, *Principles of Political Economy* (New York: Augustus M. Kelly, 1965), bk. 4, ch. 2, secs. 4 and 5, pp. 705-8. See also *The Bible*, Old Testament, Genesis 37-48, The Story of Joseph.

The basic proposition of the classical theory of speculation—that speculators make money if, and only if, their activities stabilize prices—is "too strong to hold with any great generality." See M. J. Farrell, "Profitable Speculation," *Economica*, vol. 33 (1966). Goss and Yamey, commenting (in "Introduction: The Economics of Futures Trading") on Farrell's paper, indicate that this basic proposition "was critically dependent for its *general* validity upon certain conditions (for example that the non-speculative demand function and the reigning price in any period are independent of speculative activity in earlier periods, and that the excess demand function of non-speculators is linear)." However, the introduction of speculators' transaction costs and their costs of carrying an open position (including finance and storage costs as well as costs of bearing uncertainty) lead to less stringent sufficient conditions. Cf. Farrell, "Profitable Speculation," and Goss and Yamey, "Introduction: The Economics of Futures Trading."

Thus, whether or not successful (unsuccessful) speculation is stabilizing (destabilizing) is an empirical issue. This writer is not aware of any evidence in support of the argument that successful speculation is destabilizing. The 1973-1974 fluctuation in commodity prices has been mentioned as a possible case. Empirical evidence does not appear to support this possibility. See Roger W. Gray and David J. S. Rutledge, "The Role of Short Speculation in the Futures Markets," unpublished manuscript prepared for the Chicago Board of Trade, 1978.

The cost of holding inventories includes several elements: storage cost, possible deterioration of quality, possible fire or theft (if not covered by insurance), financing costs (internal or external), and the risk of price change. These costs differ among assets, and the differences help to explain why some markets have become more liquid than others.

Assets that are subject to little or no deterioration with the passage of time and whose value is high in relation to bulk usually have low carrying costs. This helps to explain the early development of liquid markets for some durable commodities, especially the precious metals, and for securities. In contrast, the practicability of holding inventories in nondurables, such as fresh fruit, or in durables whose value is low in relation to bulk, such as bricks, is severely limited, thereby inhibiting the development of liquid markets.

Any of the elements of the cost of holding inventories are subject to reduction. Better storage facilities developed as increased demand permitted economies of scale to be realized. In addition, the benefits of greater storage capability have encouraged technological improvements designed to enhance the durability of products. For example, the development of refrigeration made products such as eggs, broilers, orange juice, and pork bellies more durable, thereby improving the liquidity of their markets.

Insurance services have reduced the cost from possible fire or theft of inventories. Such services were developed as increased demand made economies of scale possible through the pooling of risk. In addition, the development and enforcement of property rights have reduced the risk of possible theft and therefore the cost of theft insurance.

Although there have been improvements in storage facilities and in devices for reducing theft, the actual cost of storage and incidence of theft appear to have increased. This development should not be surprising. The effect of inflation on storage costs appears to have more than offset the greater efficiency in storage technology; the effects of a more permissive judiciary and new technologies, including the spread of the computer industry, on the rates of return from theft may well have more than offset the effects of improved devices for reducing theft.

The two elements of carrying cost that have been the most difficult to reduce are the uncertainty attaching to future spot prices and the costs of financing. These elements of carrying cost are closely related: the higher the risk of price uncertainty, the higher the financing costs, *ceteris paribus*.

Both price uncertainty and financing costs work against speculative as well as commercial demand for holding inventories. Indeed, although inventories may be held in the expectation of favorable price developments, these expectations cannot be held with certainty. Speculators in inventory holdings presumably have a comparative advantage in predicting the future course of prices. However, as is the case with commercial demand, price uncertainty reduces speculative demand (*ceteris paribus*).

Historically, the risk of price uncertainty attached to inventory holdings, together with the costs of financing them, served to limit the volume of such holdings. And this limited the benefits that specialization of functions and attendant economies of scale could bring. There developed a tendency to diversify, rather than specialize, production and inventory holdings in order to reduce the risk of price uncertainty and financing costs. Diversifying production and inventory holdings, however, tends to be less operationally efficient than specializing. Further, diversification could not always appreciably reduce risk and financing costs because of covariation of commodity prices.

The price risk and financing costs inherent in specialized production and inventory holdings became prime factors in the economic demand for contracts for future transactions. And the dramatic increase in price risk and financing costs during the post–World War II period is in part responsible for the immense recent increase in the demand for such contracts.

Orderly Market Conditions. The absence of monopolies, deliberately false rumors, and destabilizing trading activity fosters orderly market conditions.

Monopolies. Market liquidity is an important contributor to competition, and thereby to orderly market conditions. Liquidity reduces the cost of information to market participants (actual and prospective) and makes it unlikely that one or a few firms will dominate the issuance of market information. In this way, liquidity helps to prevent structural monopolies and price manipulation.

An absence of artificial barriers to market entry also fosters competition. In this connection, it may be important that numerous traders—foreign as well as domestic—participate in a market. It may also be important, however, that sources of information—foreign as well as domestic, and governmental as well as private—be unencumbered by monopolistic restrictions. In this way, relevant information can be brought to bear on a market's price.

Deliberately false rumors. Artificial barriers to market information allow the circulation of deliberately false rumors. In particular, uncertainty based on lack of access to, or on doubts about the quality of, a monopolist's information feeds deliberately false rumors. This uncertainty typically manifests itself in wide bid-asked price spreads—both at the margin and in the whole structure of quotations. The dissemination of deliberately false rumors often tends to broaden the price spreads.

Governmental monopoly of information is a particularly troublesome problem. Governmental policy vacillation and the restriction of information about the parameters affecting policy making are conducive to the dissemination of deliberately false rumors.

The perceived quality of information released by an entity, such as government, that has a monopoly on some types of information also has a bearing on rumors. A history of governmental inaction, of large or surprising changes in policy, or of factual inaccuracies causes skepticism about new information, and this fosters the spread of rumors. In this respect, the aftereffects of fiscal and monetary excesses as well as governmental corruption in the United States and elsewhere may persist for many years, perhaps decades.

A deliberately false rumor is most viable when it is difficult to contradict. Complex governmental deliberations on a subject create such situations. For example, while the government deliberated on the financial crisis of New York City in 1975, a rumor was spread that the chairman of the Federal Reserve Board was going to bail out the city. The rumor also indicated that the chairman would, of course, deny the report. Temporarily, this rumor had a pronounced effect on the prices of the city's outstanding debt securities.

Destabilizing trading activity. Destabilizing trading activity may result from insufficient market use rather than from excessive speculative trading. Insufficiency of trading may exist because of restrictions on short positions, limitations on speculative positions, or limitations on daily price movements. Removal of such restrictions would improve the working of the market by releasing the full forces of demand and supply.

Market Organization. The organization of a market is inherently related to its liquidity. In particular, the enhancement of market liquidity serves to foster the development of an organized market: such organization can then realize economies of scale. In turn, many aspects of improved market organization, such as low margin requirements and clearinghouses, promote market liquidity.

25

Development of a market's organization involves applying economies of scale to effecting transactions as well as to providing information about the terms of transactions. In particular, organized markets usually come into existence in response to the economic demand of traders who make frequent transactions in a particular asset. Often, dealers are the catalysts that bring an organized market into existence. With the passage of time, however, dealers frequently delegate direct management of an organized market to appointed managers. By becoming members of the exchange, dealers retain a supervisory role.

The history of a market's organization is one of increasing specialization of function induced by, and in turn inducing, an increase in market liquidity. The markets for some agricultural commodities provide a case in point.

Prior to the nineteenth century, limitations in transportation and communication were such that agricultural markets were predominantly local in nature. The many local markets that existed were small and not well integrated with one another. Differences in demand-supply conditions in the various local markets often kept the prices of similar products far apart. These local markets had only rudimentary systems for effecting transactions and providing price information. Prices typically were arrived at through the time-consuming process of bargaining and negotiation on each transaction. Agricultural producers usually were directly involved in the price determination process.

In the nineteenth century, the local spot markets for commodities became less important as central markets were organized. Technological advances in transportation (the railroad) and communication (the telegraph and telephone) as well as in production (including storage facilities) fostered an increase of demand and economies of scale in production. Soon the economic demands of producers, consumers, and dealers for more efficient systems of effecting transactions and of collecting and disseminating price information led to the centralization of transactions in terminal markets, such as in Chicago and New York.

The development of a market between the grain-producing, livestock-producing, and dairy-producing sections of the country and many of the processing and consuming sections was a natural development. Chicago had an advantage over other Midwest locations because of its easy access to low-cost transportation. Similarly, New York became the center for transactions in world-traded commodities.

A large market has an inherent advantage over a small market: the larger number of participants means that asset liquidity will be greater. Once started, the process of market centralization may take on a life of its own. The large volume of commodity transactions in a centralized market tends to give it a high degree of liquidity. In turn, high liquidity stimulates further use of the market.

The development of central markets also integrated the non-central markets. Arbitrage transactions between local and central markets brought about greater uniformity of the prices of similar transactions among markets at a given point in time.

The price information system in the centralized markets became considerably more impersonal and specialized than it had been in the local markets. Agricultural producers took a much less active role in the pricing process. The more developed pricing system that was emerging enabled agricultural producers to concentrate their attention on their field of expertise—namely, agricultural output. Intermediaries in the form of dealers and brokers facilitated the separation of commodity producer and commodity purchaser. Increasingly, intermediaries took over the process of search, contract negotiations, drawing up and enforcing agreements, and physical transfer of goods.

One type of central market, the organized commodity exchange, generally developed in the largest and most strategically located of the central markets. The exchanges were a means of applying economies of scale to systems of collecting and disseminating information and of effecting transactions.

During the twentieth century—after World War I and especially after World War II—several developments in transportation (the expansion of the highway system and the increased efficiency of truck transportation) and communication (the growth of communication by radio) helped to transform the centralized system of marketing agricultural products into a more decentralized one.[22] Improvements in the system of price information (the increased application of standardization, the expansion of the government's market-news reporting services, and the development and increased role of futures markets) enabled the decentralized markets to operate more efficiently.

Market organization—including exchanges, brokers, inspection services—has developed in securities as well as commodity markets. Many of the most advanced features of market organization are found in futures markets. This is not surprising in view of the high liquidity of futures markets, which usually improves the quality of market organization. Unlike securities markets, in whose operations inside

---

[22] Cf. Frederick L. Thomsen and Richard J. Foote, *Agricultural Prices,* Second Edition (New York: McGraw-Hill, 1952), ch. 8.

information is inherent, futures markets make available to all, on practically equal terms, information about the assets traded.[23] The openness, or public nature, of futures markets is conducive to high liquidity and thus to developed market organization.

Improving the quality of market organization and mitigating disorderly markets are the two principal roles of government regulation designed to improve the orderliness (operating efficiency) of markets. Thus, the quality of market organization and the orderliness of market conditions must be considered in the context of government regulation.

Interrelationship of the Elements of Efficiency. The three aspects of market efficiency—the liquidity of the market, the orderliness of market conditions, and the character of market organization—are mutually reinforcing. Earlier, the discussion focused on the effects of market liquidity on the other two aspects; this discussion focuses on the effects of market conditions and market organization on liquidity.

There are long-run as well as short-run problems with disorderly market conditions. The short-run problem consists of inefficient allocation of resources because of inefficient or misleading price information. If persistent, this situation becomes a serious long-run problem. A market's participants learn to recognize actual or potential disorderly conditions and lose confidence in information emanating from the market. As a result, in the long run, the liquidity of the market is impaired.

The disorderly foreign exchange market of the early 1970s illustrates this sequence. The international value of the U.S. dollar was being pegged at an unrealistic level by a monopolist—the U.S. government—and the price information generated in this market was misleading. During this period, the liquidity of the foreign exchange market deteriorated—first in the forward market, with the increasing spreads in bid-asked price quotations and shorter maturities that were rather widely reported, and later in the spot market for foreign exchange. The Bretton Woods system of adjustable pegged exchange rates finally broke down in 1973 (see Appendix A).

---

[23] It is useful to recognize that inside information should exist in securities markets. Indeed, inside information provides an incentive for innovation. However, inside information also serves to augment investors' uncertainty about quality of individual security issues. The crucial issue is thus not whether inside information should exist, but rather how much and under what conditions it should exist. The Securities and Exchange Commission plays a vital role in this area.

Disorderly market conditions thus generate a reduced demand for the services of the market, and may—unless the sources of the problems are removed—dissolve the market. Even if the market survives, it will be less liquid and have a reduced role as a market. A wider separation of bid and asked price quotations tends to develop throughout the whole structure of such quotations.

In addition to the reaction of the market's participants to perceived disorderly conditions, the government (Congress, the administration, or regulatory agencies) might also react. The governmental reaction might well take the form of attempting to remove the symptoms of the problem rather than its source. This reaction might only serve to worsen still further the existing market situation.

The role of a market's organization—in particular, the functions of institutions, such as brokerage firms and even exchanges, that service a market—have often been misunderstood. These institutions are sometimes viewed as parasites that lower the prices paid to producers and raise the prices paid by consumers. Actually, these institutions perform a useful economic function: they enhance market liquidity by facilitating transactions and by providing information relevant to such transactions. The exchanges, for example, have been instrumental in improving the quality of spot price quotations by centralizing information on terms of transactions, grading products, and enforcing contractual obligations. Brokers reduce search, transportation, transfer, and other transaction costs facing market participants. The reduction of per unit transaction costs serves to generate an increased volume of transactions.

One reason that these institutions' economic roles are sometimes misunderstood is that their service often entails a substitution of objective costs for the subjective costs that otherwise would be borne by one or both parties to an exchange. The objective costs must be lower than those that the parties to an exchange would incur by dealing directly with one another—otherwise, the service would not continue to exist.

3

Forward and Futures Markets

Markets for future transactions are markets for contracts to future spot transactions. Such markets entail a means of effecting contracts to future transactions in an asset (or service) as well as a way of collecting and disseminating information on the terms of such contracts.

Market forces determine both the types of contracts for future transactions and the maturity limits of these contracts. In addition, market forces determine why some markets for future transactions are highly liquid, while others are low in liquidity. It should be recognized, however, that market forces operate in a particular institutional framework, including regulatory and other governmental policies.

Types of Contracts and Markets

Contracts for future spot transactions may be of two types. First, such contracts may consist of rights and obligations to spot transactions in the future. Second, such contracts may consist (for purchasers) of rights—but not obligations—to such transactions. The second type of contract is referred to as an option contract and is considered in the next chapter.

The first type of contract, usually regarded as the conventional one, requires the making or taking of delivery of an asset in the future. In particular, the contract is an agreement to buy or sell a stated quantity of an asset (or service) of given quality for delivery (or rental) at a future date (or over a period of time) at a specified price (or with some provision for its specification). Most such contracts also name the delivery point (or points) where the future transaction will take place.

A contract governing rights and obligations to a future spot transaction conceivably could be made for any asset or service. Often, such contracts provide for the simultaneous exchange of an asset and money at a future date. There are, however, a wide variety of cases in which such simultaneity does not exist. For example, many contracts for future transactions, such as those for services, may consist of an agreement today to render a service over a period of time (beginning at some date in the future) for a payment or series of payments (that also begins in the future). In addition, some contracts have both spot and future elements. For example, the issuance of a bond normally entails the exchange of a specified amount of money today for the promise of a series of interest payments and repayment of principal in the future.

Contracts involving rights and obligations to future spot transactions may or may not be traded on markets; and the markets, in turn, may or may not be organized. Markets for future spot transactions in assets usually are more developed than those in services, because it is easier to define the quality of assets than of services.

In fact, markets for future transactions in services are not likely to be well developed unless the quality of the services to be rendered is reasonably homogeneous. Such homogeneity in quality can occur only in situations in which there is little individualization in the services to be provided. Except for some blue collar work, such situations are rare. The difficulty of enforcing service contracts also discourages the development of markets for future services.

The earliest markets for future transactions were "forward" markets in which two parties negotiated a tailor-made contract; records of such contracts and markets can be traced at least as far back as the seventeenth century. Subsequently, highly organized, or "futures," markets emerged.

Futures markets, the most widely known markets for contracts to future spot transactions, operate through organized exchanges. Indeed, regulation of futures markets prohibits the trading of formal futures contracts off the exchanges. Contracts traded in futures markets provide for agreement today to deliver (a short position), or take delivery of (a long position), a specified grade and quantity of an asset at a specified location(s) and time(s) in the future at a price negotiated and stipulated through auction arrangements.

Futures markets emerged in the nineteenth century. The volume of futures trading and the level of open interest (contracts outstanding) have been greatest in the United States and England. Futures markets currently exist for a wide array of real and financial assets, including grains and feeds, livestock, industrial raw materials, precious metals, foods, financial instruments, and foreign currencies. Although commodities and securities differ, futures markets for commodities and securities are similar; in particular, the factors that foster their development are much the same, and so are the economic benefits that they provide. For this reason, the economic rationale for the regulation of futures markets—whatever the underlying asset—is much the same.

The sequence of development of futures markets roughly parallels —with a time lag—that of organized spot markets. The earliest futures markets were for agricultural commodities, industrial raw materials, and precious metals. Later, futures markets developed for semi-processed products (such as plywood). Recently, futures markets have developed for foreign currencies and for financial assets.

The last two decades have witnessed a dramatic increase in the types of contracts traded, and in the volume of transactions and open interest. In the United States, the volume of transactions in futures increased from less than 4 million contracts in 1960 to over 50 million contracts in 1978 (the dollar volume of assets represented by the contracts traded in 1978 was about two trillion dollars); and the average open interest increased from about 140,000 contracts in 1960 to about 1,370,000 contracts in 1978.

The recent increase in use of futures reflects, in part, increased commercial demand occasioned by the larger volume of exposed positions in spot markets together with higher price risks and financing costs. It also reflects the increased willingness of speculators to participate in such markets occasioned, *inter alia*, by the increased commercial demand. Appendix B describes a recently popular use of futures contracts for delaying and reducing tax payments.

Additional Aspect of Market Efficiency

The efficiency of markets for future transactions relates to the ease of effecting transactions and to the quality of information that they provide. Like the efficiency of spot markets, the efficiency of forward and futures markets is a function of the liquidity of the assets traded, the orderliness of market conditions, and the quality of the markets' organization. The concept of efficiency of markets for future transactions contains, however, an additional aspect which derives from their multidimensional nature.

In effect, there are two elements—the observed and unobserved— of forward and futures markets. The observed element consists of prices (or price quotations), volume of transactions, and open interest in these markets; the unobserved element relates to expectations about spot prices (and, more broadly, spot markets) in the future. The additional aspect of these markets' efficiency consists of the quality of information that the observed element—reported daily in the *Wall Street Journal* for most futures markets—conveys about the unobserved element, particularly about expected future spot prices.

The observed and unobserved elements of a market for future transactions typically diverge; they are, however, inextricably interrelated. Improvement of information about the unobserved element has fostered the development of actual, or observed elements of, markets. In turn, the development of actual markets (in size and efficiency) has served to convey information about the unobserved element.

The efficiency of forward or futures prices as estimators of future spot prices depends on the closeness between the two prices and the confidence attached to the expected price difference. A forward or futures price normally is different from the spot price expected to prevail in the future. This difference is attributable to the typical predominance of hedging on one side of the market and the positive cost of speculation on the other (to be discussed). In an efficient market, however, this price difference is small and can be predicted with some degree of confidence. Usually, the more closely the forward or futures price estimates the future spot price, the stronger will be the confidence in the estimate. The greater the efficiency with which forward or futures prices serve as estimators of future spot prices, the better (*ceteris paribus*) is the quality of information imparted by markets for future transactions.

It should be noted that the efficiency with which forward or futures prices estimate future spot prices cannot easily be discerned by comparing forward or futures prices with the corresponding, subsequent (or realized) spot prices. There are usually wide discrepancies between current forward prices and the spot prices that actually materialize. However, during the passage of time, new types of information may appear and the evaluation of existing information may change. In addition, there may be instances in which a current forward or futures price represents something of a compromise between two or more plausible neighborhoods of future spot prices (that is, two or more modes of an expected distribution), each of which is predicated on a different assumption about a governmental policy decision that could be taken in a relevant area. Furthermore, because of the premiums typically embedded in forward and futures prices, such prices are likely to change as the maturity date of the contract approaches. Indeed, the magnitude of the premiums tends to diminish with the passage of time—approaching zero with the approach of the contract's maturity date.

Factors Conducive to Market Efficiency

This section examines factors affecting the emergence and increasing efficiency of markets for future transactions. The primary focus is on private forces as they affect the efficiency of a market. The first part deals with the role of market participants; and the second part, the market organization. The separate discussions are for analytical convenience only; they should not obscure the inherent relationship of the participants and the market organization.

For a market for future transactions in a given asset to develop, there must be the expectation of a reasonably strong and persistent commercial demand for such transactions. A necessary, but not sufficient, condition for this expectation has been the existence of a reasonably well-developed spot market for the asset: such a spot market tends to foster a demand for contracts for future transactions as well as to facilitate the production of such contracts.

Once a spot market for a particular asset becomes well developed, a sizable volume of output of that asset will be produced and a sizable amount of inventories will be held. These activities will create an economic demand for ways to reduce the cost of exposed positions in spot markets—particularly, the price risk and financing costs of such exposure. Contracts for future transactions are one way of meeting this demand.

Well-developed spot markets also enable contracts for future transactions to be economically feasible. Well-developed spot markets foster conditions conducive to the emergence of forward and futures contracts in several ways: the standardization of asset quality in spot markets tends to reduce the cost of ascertaining the quality of an asset for future delivery; good spot price information facilitates the formation of expectations about future spot prices; and the very existence of a spot market organization reduces the start-up costs of an organized market for future transactions.

Role of Market Participants. The demand for forward and futures contracts comes from commercial firms and speculators.[1] An exposed

---

[1] The analysis in this section is based on material in the author's earlier study, *Accounting Standards and International Finance: With Special Reference to Multinationals* (Washington, D.C.: American Enterprise Institute, 1976).

position in a spot market together with uncertainty about spot prices are the foundation of commercial demand for contracts for future transactions. Production and marketing of assets require that producers and dealers assume exposed positions in spot markets; and price uncertainty is inherent in a dynamic economy—especially for those assets whose supply cannot be varied by rapid and extensive changes in the rate of production. The prices of such assets tend to fluctuate rapidly with changes in demand or with exogenous changes in supply (especially where the demand schedules are inelastic).[2]

Commercial firms and speculative investors seek to reduce the risk of exposed positions (actual or anticipated) in spot markets by entering into contracts for future transactions in the same asset. For example, a grain elevator holding a certain amount of wheat will be exposed to risk because of uncertainty about the future price of wheat. The grain elevator would probably gain if the price of wheat rises, but it would lose if the price falls. To reduce this uncertainty, the grain elevator may sell a contract for future delivery of wheat. Now, if the price of spot wheat should change, the forward (or futures) price of wheat is likely to change in the same direction. As a result, the "basis" —the difference between the spot price and forward price of wheat— may not change very much. Now, the grain elevator may not gain if the price of spot wheat rises, since that gain may be offset by the loss incurred in the short position in the forward contract; however, the grain elevator may not lose if the price of spot wheat falls, since that loss may be offset by gains incurred in the short position on the forward contract. Thus, to the extent that spot and forward prices have a high positive covariation, price fluctuations that generate gains in one market produce roughly equivalent losses in the other, thereby reducing price risk.

The decisions to take an exposed position in a spot market and to attempt to offset this exposure through a contract for future transaction are related. A firm continually reviews its risk exposure and the prospects for its rate of return. The economic demand for contracts for future transactions arises from attempts by business firms to secure an optimal position with regard to risk and the rate of return.

When a commercial firm takes a position in a contract for future transaction as an offset to a spot position, it will not necessarily be in a less risky position than previously. The contract may be the vehicle for extending the firm's operations, and this may result in expanded risk as well as new profit opportunities. However, the firm's

---

[2] Cf. Alfred Marshall, *Industry and Trade* (London: Macmillan and Co., 1927), bk. 2, ch. 5, sec. 3.

new risk exposure—even if extended—will be better than it would have been without the offsetting contract for future transaction. In short, the reduction of risk exposure for a given spot position (actual or anticipated) facilitates an expansion of such positions (that is, larger inventory holdings or commodity output), making possible gains from economies of scale or from functional specialization.

Costs as well as benefits underlie the commercial demand for contracts for future transactions, however, just as in other risk-reducing devices. Typically, firms use other risk-reducing devices, including incorporation and vertical integration,[3] to achieve their optimal trade-off between risk and return. Risk has different elements which may require different solutions; then, too, expanding use of any one device may entail diminishing marginal benefits. Presumably, firms seek the least-cost method or combination of methods for hedging the price risk of exposed positions in actuals.

Commercial demand for forward contracts. The price risk of exposed positions (actual or anticipated) in actuals may be hedged through offsetting positions in forward or futures contracts. The benefits of hedging entail reduction of the cost of exposure to price uncertainty. Thus, it is important to consider the meaning of the "cost of exposure," and the way in which hedging reduces such cost, as well as the cost of hedging.

A firm's cost of exposure to price uncertainty in a particular asset depends on its net position (actual or anticipated) in the asset, the period during which this position is expected to exist, the expected level and variability of the asset's price during that period (including the confidence attached thereto), the degree to which the firm's asset position is effectively diversified, and the firm's attitude toward risk (that is, the degree of its risk aversion). As a result of differences in one or more of these factors, the cost of exposure for a given asset will differ among firms, and for a given firm over time. The cost of exposure will also vary among assets because of differences in price behavior and in the nature (including duration) of their production and marketing processes.

The hedging of price risk of actuals—through offsetting positions in contracts for future transactions—reduces the cost of exposure,

---

[3] Vertical integration of production processes is not necessarily harmful to the development of markets, as is often assumed. To be sure, such development may directly weaken one link in the chain of a given market (from raw material to consumer goods). The bypass of one link, however, may—through increased transactions—strengthen subsequent and prior links. And this development may indirectly strengthen market development in the bypassed link. It is not impossible that the indirect effects may at times outweigh the direct effects.

because the difference between spot and forward prices (the basis) is typically less variable than the level of the spot price. It is, however, virtually impossible to eliminate the cost of price risk exposure entirely. The price of a contract for a future transaction will generally move in the same direction as the price of the corresponding actual, but it will rarely do so by the same amount. Indeed, although the difference between spot and forward prices (the basis) may be more predictable than the level of the spot price, the basis too is uncertain. The expected benefits of hedging depend on the degree to which the basis is more predictable than the level of the spot price, and this expectation is likely to differ among firms and for a given firm over time.

Typically, diminishing benefits are associated with added increments of hedging. In part, this may be because large exposed positions entail higher marginal risks than small exposed ones; in part, this may reflect uncertainty about the magnitude of exposure. This latter situation is likely to exist for growers or producers of a commodity whose total output (and hence total exposure) is not known with certainty.

A reduced risk of exposure sometimes has an important side effect—namely, lower financing costs facing the commercial firm. For example, rates on bank loans are at times lower if hedging has reduced exposure to risk.[4]

The cost of this type of hedging consists of transaction costs and the cost of carrying a position in a forward contract. As with the benefits of hedging, the expected cost of hedging a particular exposed position typically differs both among firms and for a given firm over time. Such differences stem from differences in transaction costs or in the cost (actual or perceived) of carrying a position in a forward contract.

Transaction costs include costs associated with the negotiation of a contract and its subsequent termination (through maturation, sale, or offset). In addition, and usually of greater significance, transaction costs include extensive and intensive search costs. Extensive search aims to secure a favorable price on a given type of forward contract; intensive search seeks to assure the quality of a given forward contract—both the asset to be transferred and the other party to the transaction.

The carrying cost of a forward contract includes opportunity costs, the risk of default on the contract, and the prospective change

---

[4] Appropriate bank financing of hedged positions usually entails the financing of additions to margins that the movement of forward prices may require; such price movements usually have little effect on the economic position of the hedged firm. It is unfortunate that so few banks today appear to recognize this point.

in the premium embedded in the asset's forward price. Opportunity costs consist of returns foregone in other uses while funds are tied up in the hedging operation. The lower the margin requirements for taking a position in a forward or futures contract, the less this cost will be. Usually, margin requirements on forward and futures contracts are quite low.

There are two types of default risk included in the cost of hedging: the default risk facing the hedging firm, and that facing the other party to the forward contract. The cost of default risk facing the hedging firm depends on the perceived quality of the other party to the forward contract (including the confidence attached thereto) and on the prospective cost of contract enforcement. The cost of default risk of the other type is included in the hedger's payment necessary to induce the other party to take a position in a forward contract; this payment takes the form of a premium embedded in the price of the forward contract.

The premium (or discount) embedded in a forward contract price consists of the difference between the forward price of an asset at a given point in time and the spot price of the corresponding asset expected to be realized in the future. The possibility of the hedging firm's default is included in the premium required by the other party to the transaction. When the contract is held to maturity, the entire premium is a cost to the hedging firm. As the contract approaches maturity, the size of the premium tends to diminish.

The magnitude of the premium (discount) is determined by demand-supply conditions in the market for future transactions; that is, the premium often is determined by commercial demand for short positions (to hedge long exposed positions in spot markets) and the cost to speculative investors of taking long positions.

The volume of a commercial firm's hedging is continually changing. The volume of hedging depends on perceived benefits and costs, and these perceptions are continually changing. Many firms choose not to hedge at all. Sometimes, a commercial firm's expectation of future spot prices differs from that of the market. For example, a firm with a long exposed position in the spot market may expect the future spot price of an asset to be substantially higher than the prevailing quotation for a forward contract in that asset. In this case, the firm would favor an exposed position and view with disfavor the hedging of such a position. Even when the benefits of hedging are positive, the costs may appear to be too high to justify it.

Emergence and development of forward contracts. The early forward markets developed in response to commercial demand for a way to offset the risk of long exposure in actuals. At a later stage, speculative investors in actuals also sometimes sought short positions in forward markets in order to reduce the risk of their long exposure in actuals.[5]

The commercial demand for short positions in forward contracts came primarily from two sources: dealers whose inventory holdings (actual or expected) were large relative to their sales commitments (actual or expected), and producers of staple raw materials whose output (actual or expected) was large relative to their sales commitments (actual or expected). As trade expanded, larger output and inventory holdings followed, and the larger risks and financing costs associated with this increased activity led to a greater demand for hedging.

There is much evidence that commercial demand for forward contracts preceded speculative demand.[6] However, the precedence of commercial demand over speculation in forward markets is more a matter of logic than of actual sequence. With hedging demand largely or entirely on one side of the market (usually the short side in earlier

---

[5] There is a difference in degree, not of kind, between so-called speculators and investors. For this reason, the term, "speculative investors," would appear to be more appropriate than the term, "speculators." Furthermore, because of its pejorative connotation, the term "speculators" should be used with caution. This term is frequently used in this study only because of its brevity. It is interesting that on at least one occasion in the *General Theory*, Keynes used the phrase, "speculative investors." On most (if not all) other occasions, he used the shorter version.

In this connection, Alfred Marshall stated, "most of the chief distinctions marked by economic terms are differences not of kind but of degree. At first sight they appear to be differences of kind, and to have sharp outlines which can be clearly marked out; but a more careful study has shown that there is no real breach of continuity. It is a fact that the progress of economics has discovered hardly any new real differences in kind, while it is continually resolving apparent differences in kind into differences in degree." [From Alfred Marshall, *Principles of Economics*, Ninth Edition (New York: Macmillan Co., 1961), p. 52.]

[6] See Roger W. Gray and David J. S. Rutledge, "The Economics of Commodity Futures Markets: A Survey," *Review of Marketing and Agricultural Economics*, vol. 39, no. 4 (December 1971), pp. 57-108, esp. pp. 58-63. Gray and Rutledge state, "It is first of all clear that futures trading grew out of the merchandising trade already in existence." [References are here made to H. S. Irwin, *Evolution of Futures Trading* (Madison, Wisconsin: Mimir Publishers, Inc., 1954); C. H. Taylor, *History of the Board of Trade of the City of Chicago* (Chicago: Robert O. Law Co., 1917); and H. Working, "Economic Functions of Futures Markets," in H. Bakken, ed., *Futures Trading in Livestock—Origins and Concepts* (Madison, Wisconsin: Mimir Publishers, Inc., 1970)]. Gray and Rutledge continue, "Merchants, dealers, processors, etc., the regular tradespeople, organized the markets to better facilitate the trading they were already engaged in. An alternative possibility—that they might have been organized by persons outside the trade who were desirous of speculating in price movements—finds no historical support" (p. 58).

decades), a viable forward market would need to have speculative investors, or speculators, on the opposite side of the market willing to assume positions at prices acceptable to hedgers.[7]

Speculators are, in effect, providing insurance to hedgers—through the assumption of the risk of price volatility—and they must receive sufficient compensation to be willing to provide this service. Indeed, speculators will not take an open position unless they receive what they consider sufficient compensation.

As Keynes has pointed out, the cost of providing insurance against price risk is typically "very high, much higher than is charged for any other form of insurance, though perhaps it is inevitable that a risk which only averages out over units spread *through time* should be less easy to insure than one which averages out over units which are nearly simultaneous—for we have to wait too long for the actuarial result."[8] The cost to speculators of providing this insurance to commercial firms includes transaction costs as well as the costs of carrying an open position in a forward contract. The latter consist of storage or safekeeping costs (which are very low, because it is easy to store a piece of paper), opportunity costs (which are usually very low or zero because of small margin requirements), and costs of bearing the risk of an open position including the risk of default (the principal element of speculators' cost).

The price charged by speculators for providing insurance against price risk is the difference between the current forward price of an asset and the future spot price of the asset that they expect will materialize. This price is designed to cover the speculators' transaction and carrying costs (including a rate of return for their entrepreneurial activity). To be sure, speculators cannot make money unless there are others (commercial firms) who are willing to lose money in the sense of paying for insurance. The more entities (commercial firms) that are willing to pay for the insurance that speculators provide, and the greater the entities' sense of urgency, the higher the prospective spec-

---

[7] In this connection, Holbrook Working has shown for several markets that speculative open interest tends to respond closely and quickly to the volume of commercial firms' open interest rather than the other way around. See Holbrook Working, "Speculation on Hedging Markets," *Food Research Institute Studies*, vol. 1 (May 1960). See, also, B. A. Goss and B. S. Yamey, "Introduction: The Economics of Futures Trading," in B. A. Goss and B. S. Yamey, eds., *The Economics of Futures Trading* (New York: Halstead Press, 1976). Indeed, increases in commercial demand for forward (or futures) contracts tend to augment the returns to speculators through changes in forward prices, thereby inducing a greater volume of speculation.

[8] J. M. Keynes, "Some Aspects of Commodity Markets," *The Manchester Guardian*, March 29, 1923; emphasis in original.

ulative returns will tend to become and, hence, the larger the volume of speculation.

Thus, the crucial issue regarding the viability of many forward contracts and markets—particularly those of earlier times—is the strength of hedgers' demands for short positions compared with the willingness of speculators (on balance) to assume the risk of open long positions. For certain types of forward contracts—in fresh fruit, for example—the strength of hedgers' demands has simply not been sufficient to induce speculators to enter the market. The same is true of all forward contracts having distant maturities. In these situations, the maximum price that hedgers have been willing to pay for insurance has been less than the minimum price that speculators have been willing to charge for providing this service.

In the early forward markets, because of the preponderance of commercial demand for short positions, the expected future spot price was in general higher than the current forward price. Such a price relationship may exist whether the expected spot price is above or below the current spot price. Therefore, if the future spot price is expected to be approximately the same as the current spot price, the current forward price will be below the current spot price. Keynes believed that in normal conditions the current and expected spot prices would be roughly the same. This belief was the pillar of his theory of "normal backwardation"—the excess of spot price over forward price in normal conditions.[9] Keynes's theory might also be described as one of "average backwardation," since what is normal in a commodity market may be expectations of large price movements rather than roughly constant prices.

Over time, the commercial demand for long positions in contracts for future transactions has increased. This development appears to stem from the increase of sales commitments by dealers and the expansion of "fixprice markets," or "customers' markets." Dealers whose sales commitments (actual or anticipated) exceed current inventories (actual or anticipated) have an exposed short position; and manufacturers whose resource inputs (actual or anticipated) fall short of those necessary for future "fixed price" sales (actual or expected) also have an exposed short position. Both may seek to reduce their short exposure through an offsetting long position in contracts for future transactions.

An increase of dealers' sales commitments relative to their inventories may be attributable to an increased regularity of purchase orders

---

[9] See J. M. Keynes, *A Treatise on Money*, vol. 2 (New York: Harcourt, Brace, and Co., 1930), pp. 142-44.

from foreign or domestic manufacturers who are seeking to assure continuity in resource supplies and output. The increase of fixprice markets may be attributable to the growing importance of brand-name products and the attendant benefits of short-run price stability.[10]

Although the average backwardation of forward (or futures) prices in relation to spot prices is probably less pervasive now than in earlier times, backwardation (on average) probably still exists for most assets. At least two factors appear to contribute to this condition. First, because of technical rigidities in the production process, the commodity producer ordinarily has a greater risk exposure than the commodity user.[11] Both are faced by a trade-off between technical efficiency and risk exposure. However, market conditions facing the commodity user are likely to be such that his optimal technology is less specialized than that of the commodity producer. Stated differently, the flexibility (substitutability) of resource use is typically greater for the commodity user than the producer. For this reason, the risk exposure facing the commodity producer is likely to be greater than that facing the commodity user, and thus the benefits of hedging are likely to be greater for the producer. As a result, the economic demand by commercial firms for short positions in forward contracts is likely to be stronger than their demand for long positions.

This conclusion is based on a *ceteris paribus* assumption about the relationship between spot and forward prices. In fact, however, everything else generally is not equal. Apart from very temporary market disturbances, the ability to purchase assets and hold them for delivery on a forward contract (negotiated at the same time that the spot position was taken) sets an upper limit to the amount by which the forward price may exceed the spot price of an asset. In particular, the forward price can exceed the spot price only up to the cost of the above arbitrage transaction—the total of transaction costs, storage costs, insurance costs, possible deterioration of quality, financing costs, and the competitive return to arbitrage transactions in the spot and forward markets. Because the cost of arbitrage is likely to vary from one firm to another, the cost that would set the upper limit to this price differential would be that for marginal firms—those whose cost would be such that they would be indifferent between entering or not entering into arbitrage transactions in the spot and forward markets. The upper limit to the price differential varies from one asset to

---

[10] Cf. J. R. Hicks, *Economic Perspectives: Further Essays on Money and Growth* (Oxford: Oxford University Press, 1977), esp. the preface.

[11] See J. R. Hicks, *Value and Capital* (Oxford: The Clarendon Press, 1939), p. 137.

another because of differences in any of the arbitrage costs, such as susceptibility to quality deterioration.

The existence of an upper limit to the amount by which the forward price can exceed the spot price without—for practical purposes—any corresponding lower limit creates an asymmetry in the expected benefits of long and short hedging.[12] To the extent that the forward price exceeds the spot price by the cost of arbitrage in the spot and forward markets, the potential short hedger has an advantage over the potential long hedger: if the spot-forward price relationship were to change, it could only narrow, which would be to the advantage of the short hedger and to the disadvantage of the long hedger. This asymmetry of expected benefits of hedging may well lead to a greater volume of short than of long hedging and a correspondingly greater volume of long than of short speculation. Empirical studies, in fact, have suggested a positive relationship between the volume of short hedging and the degree to which the forward price exceeds the spot price.[13] The asymmetry of price expectations and of expected benefits of long and short hedging is thus a second factor that may contribute to backwardation.

The relative weakness of long commercial positions in forward contracts does not, however, apply to foreign currency. In these forward markets, it is impossible to say which is the long position—it depends on the currency at which one is looking. Stated differently, "backwardation" and "forwardation" are not mutually exclusive; rather, both conditions are—in a sense—always in existence. Hedging demand generally occurs on both sides of these markets, although usually the strength of the hedging demand will be greater on one side than on the other.[14]

For most types of forward contracts, the relative strength of hedging demand for short positions varies among contracts of different maturities. Indeed, backwardation may exist on average over certain forward maturities of a particular asset while forwardation exists on average over other maturities. In fact, there may even be more than one "cross" in the maturity structure of relative hedging strengths.

Furthermore, the relative strengths of hedging demands over different forward maturities of a given asset are susceptible to change.

---

[12] See Hendrick S. Houthakker, "Normal Backwardation," in J. N. Wolfe, ed., *Value, Capital, and Growth: Essays in Honour of Sir John Hicks* (Edinburgh: Edinburgh University Press, 1968).

[13] See Goss and Yamey, "Introduction: The Economics of Futures Trading," pp. 22-23.

[14] See Hicks, *Value and Capital*, pp. 137-38, and Burns, *Accounting Standards*, pp. 39-41.

When there are strong hedging interests on both sides of a forward market, the premiums (discounts) can change to discounts (premiums). The only factor stopping the forward price from moving beyond a certain point is the introduction of speculation when it becomes sufficiently profitable for speculators to enter the market. The relative strengths of hedging demands are not likely to change too quickly; hedging demands are based on the commercial properties of a market, and these properties are, in general, reasonably stable in the short run.

There has been a lot of recent discussion whether or not speculators have been making money in the forward and futures markets. In view of the above comments, one cannot say that speculators have made money in one segment of a time period and lost money in another segment, inasmuch as the assumption that they have retained a given type of open position throughout the period is not necessarily correct. Hedgers may be changing their net position during the course of the period being investigated and, as a result, so may speculators. Indeed, speculators may have made money in both segments (or lost money in both segments).

For any given period, speculators (on balance) may lose money primarily from unforeseen events and perhaps occasionally from lack of sufficient foresight. One must, however, remember that speculators can have imperfect foresight and still make money.

A large speculative interest in a market for future transactions is useful, since it serves, *inter alia*, to reduce the cost of hedging—particularly, the size of the premiums embedded in forward prices—by providing balance to a market characterized by unequal hedging strengths. In view of the fact that most markets for future transactions are characterized by stronger hedging interests on one side of the market than the other over long periods of time, speculation is essential to the viability of such markets.

Speculators, then, through their effects on liquidity, enhance the efficiency of markets for future transactions. In addition, and of significance, speculators contribute to the efficiency with which forward prices estimate future spot prices. First, speculation enhances the stability of forward prices, thereby reducing price uncertainty. Second, speculation improves the accuracy with which forward prices —for a given degree of price variability—predict future spot prices. The business of speculators—indeed, their comparative advantage—lies in forecasting price developments. Both of the above effects of speculation improve the informational content of forward prices and enhance the confidence attached to forward prices as estimators of future spot prices.

Risk transfer. In the literature on forward and futures markets, there is considerable discussion of the transfer of risk from those who wish to avoid risk (commercial firms) to those who are willing to assume risk (speculators). Implicit or explicit in much of this discussion is the belief that commercial firms and speculators have different attitudes toward risk. This belief may or may not be valid. Undoubtedly, commercial firms vary in their degree of risk aversion. Similarly, the degree of risk aversion differs among speculative investors. Whether the attitude toward risk of these two groups is different (on balance) is an empirical issue. This author is inclined to believe that, in any given economy, attitudes toward risk are much the same, on average, for speculative investors and commercial firms.

In contracts for future transactions, a transfer of risk does take place in the sense that commercial firms reduce, and speculative investors increase, their net exposed positions. At least two factors appear to underlie the transfer of risk from commercial firms to speculative investors: the principle of increasing risk, and a difference in capability of bearing risk. The principle of increasing risk posits that the cost of risk exposure not only increases with additions to exposure, but does so to an ever greater extent.[15] In practice, this principle would tend to generate a transfer of risk from commercial firms to speculators: that is, commercial firms will seek to reduce exposed positions, whereas speculators will take on newly exposed positions.

The transfer of risk may leave commercial firms and speculators with different risk exposures, which could reflect unequal capabilities of bearing risk. There are two aspects of differences in risk-bearing capability. First, and probably of primary significance, speculative investors (on balance) are likely to have a comparative advantage in predicting future spot prices. Speculators (on balance) are likely to have more and better information concerning future spot prices than do commercial firms (on balance). As a result, the cost of a given exposed position is likely to be smaller for speculators than for commercial firms, so that speculators may be willing to bear larger risk exposures than commercial firms.

Second, speculators and commercial firms will not have the same income and wealth positions. These differences may lead to differences in their ability to bear risk, and thereby to differences in their willingness to assume risk.

---

[15] See M. Kalecki, "The Principle of Increasing Risk," *Economica*, vol. 4, new series (November 1937), pp. 440-47.

It should be borne in mind that speculators, like commercial firms, are not a monolithic group. Differences exist among speculators in the cost of assuming open positions at a given point in time, just as differences exist for a given speculator at different points in time. Such cost differences may reflect differences in skills and knowledge, in income and wealth, and in attitude toward risk. For this reason, speculators may be on both sides of a given type (including maturity) of forward contract, although the balance of speculation will be on the side opposite to that of the preponderance of hedging.[16]

It should also be borne in mind that speculators may be expected to engage in selective speculation in much the same way that commercial firms engage in selective hedging. Indeed, the volume of speculation by a given entity (individual or firm) depends on perceived benefits and costs, and such perceptions are likely to be continually changing. The average period that a speculator holds a position in a forward or futures contract is considered to be quite short.

Maturity and asset composition of contracts. The magnitude of premiums embedded in most forward prices—especially, the prices in forward markets characterized by large differences in hedging strengths on the two sides of the market—reflects the willingness of speculators to assume open positions in forward contracts and the strength of commercial demand for insurance against price risk. For the premiums to be sufficient to induce speculative participation, they must cover the speculators' transactions and carrying costs (including some return on their entrepreneurial activity). Speculators' price uncertainty—a primary element of carrying cost—plays a pivotal role in determining premiums embedded in forward prices. The term structure and the asset structure of forward contracts have an important bearing on the degree of price uncertainty speculators face.

Speculators usually prefer to assume positions on contracts for near-term, rather than distant-term, future transactions. This preference is attributable to their greater ability to predict near-term prices as well as the greater volatility of such prices. The risk premiums speculators require for contracts for near-term future transactions are relatively low.

One reason that prices of distant-term future transactions are difficult to predict is that they often depend, *inter alia*, on governmental policies that have not yet been determined. And, on the basis of past experience (especially recent past experience), governmental

---

[16] See Burns, *Accounting Standards*, p. 37, note 10.

policies cannot be predicted easily. Shifts in governmental policies of industrial countries during the past decade (or two) have served to increase distant-term price uncertainty. This development has discouraged contracts for distant-term future transactions.

With regard to price uncertainty, it is useful to distinguish the risk of uncertainty about future macroeconomic price levels, or "macro price risk," from the risk of uncertainty about future relative prices, or "micro price risk." There is a positive correlation between these risks.[17]

Speculators are well aware that the macro price risk for contracts with distant maturities has a high cost. And speculators cannot insure very easily against this risk. Contracts indexed to price changes, to the extent they exist, decrease the distant-term macro risk.[18] A crucial issue, however, is whether the incremental cost to commercial firms of issuing indexed contracts is more than offset by the increased willingness of speculators to take open positions in such contracts.

Price variability is conducive to speculation because it opens up the possibility of high rates of return for a given capital position. In his treatise, *Value and Capital*, J. R. Hicks observed that short-term interest rates fluctuate more than long-term ones.[19] Long-term rates are, in effect, an average of expected short-term rates, abstracting from the cost of illiquidity (which is a function of real investors' preference for illiquid debt, lenders' risk of being illiquid, lenders' attitude toward this risk, and the efficiency of speculation).

For forward prices, a similar situation exists: forward prices tend to fluctuate more on near-term contracts than on distant-term ones. The smaller fluctuation of distant-term forward prices is attributable to greater uncertainty about spot prices expected in the distant future and to the way such expectations are formed. In estimating distant-term future spot prices, speculators are likely to examine a number of long-run price trends (even though speculators usually attach greater weights to more recent data in estimating future prices). An average of long-run trends may provide clues to the

---

[17] Cf. Richard W. Parks, "Inflation and Relative Price Variability," *Journal of Political Economy*, vol. 86, no. 1 (January/February 1978), pp. 79-95.

[18] For many years, the Gold Clause Joint Resolution of June 5, 1933, and subsequent court decisions cast doubt on the enforceability of indexed contracts, thereby constraining the development of such contracts. Recently, Congress repealed this law, and thus improved the environment for indexing contracts. Given the U.S. government's stated objective of ending the monetary role of gold (that is, to treat gold as any other commodity is treated), Congressional repeal of the gold clause was eminently desirable.

[19] Hicks, *Value and Capital*, ch. 2.

future spot price. This process of price estimation dampens the change in distant-term forward prices associated with given changes in near-term prices.

The development of more efficient markets for future transactions (as, for example, the emergence of futures markets) is likely to reduce reliance on past price trends to form estimates of future spot prices. To the extent that past prices are still used for price estimates, the more recent prices are likely to increase in importance.[20] For this reason, the price variability of contracts for future transactions is likely to increase as markets for future transactions become more efficient. Greater price variability invites more speculative participation in the market and thereby lowers risk premiums on contracts for future transactions. As a result, the maturity structure of contracts for future transactions is likely to be extended. However, any such extension is likely to be constrained by the macro price risk.

The maximum duration to maturity is usually greater for forward contracts than for futures. For most futures contracts, the maximum duration to maturity is currently about eighteen months; for futures on financial instruments and precious metals, it is somewhat greater.

The absence of distant-term futures contracts means that investors are unable to hedge their net open positions in an effective way. As a result, investment in new plant and equipment is lower than it would otherwise be. In addition, producers of industrial raw materials are not able to hedge their investments as effectively, and future output will be lower than it otherwise would be—an adverse effect for both developed and developing countries. To the extent that governmental policy contributes to the macro price risk, it also contributes to these adverse effects.

Speculators' risk premiums on forward contracts have an asset structure as well as a term structure. Assets whose prices are considered to be unpredictable will have higher risk premiums embedded in their forward prices than those whose prices are more predictable. High bid-asked spreads will typically be associated with high risk premiums—whether for forward (or futures) contracts in assets with unpredictable prices or in all contracts for distant-term transactions. Such contracts are likely to have a small open interest and a low volume of transactions.[21]

---

[20] Cf. Charles C. Cox, "Futures Trading and Market Information," *Journal of Political Economy*, vol. 84, no. 6 (December 1976), pp. 125-37.

[21] Cf. Roger Gray, "The Characteristic Bias in Some Thin Futures Markets," *Food Research Institute Studies*, November 1960.

Role of Market Organization. Markets for future transactions may be unorganized (forward markets) or organized (futures markets). This distinction, while useful, glosses over improvements in the organization of forward markets that typically precede the setting up of a futures market. Indeed, the distinction between forward and futures markets is, in essence, a difference in the degree of formality of a market's organization.

Forward markets. In early forward markets, two parties sought to reach an agreement, or contract, whose terms were suited to their individual circumstances. Delivery was usually made by the seller to the buyer at an agreed-upon future date. These two aspects of early forward contracts—the individualized nature of the contracts and the making/taking of delivery—were inextricably related. The early forward contracts frequently were informal, based on mutual confidence in the fulfillment of the contract by the other party.[22]

The increase in volume and impersonalization of forward contracts made it more difficult to obtain information on the quality of such contracts—both the quality of the asset for future delivery and the quality (financial status and integrity) of the other party to the agreement. Over the years, a number of ways were devised for reducing uncertainty about the quality of forward contracts. In particular, standardized forms replaced personal memoranda, and somewhat standardized contracts replaced the tailor-made agreements. Over time, the benefits deriving from centralization of transactors and information increased the number of forward contracts negotiated on spot exchanges. The exchanges promoted further standardization of forward contracts.

The standardization of procedures and contracts reduced uncertainty about asset quality. As a result, the markets' liquidity increased and forward contracts became more easily transferable. The parties to forward contracts used these agreements increasingly as risk-reducing devices without ever making or taking delivery of the assets involved.

Uncertainty about quality of the opposite party to a forward agreement has been more difficult to reduce than uncertainty about asset quality. The high cost of default (actual and expected) on forward contracts has militated against their liquidity. Exchanges have attempted to deal with the default problem by adopting rules for margin requirements—that is, guarantees of performance as opposed to down payments. These rules have not assured the fulfill-

---

[22] On the development of forward markets, see Irwin, *Evolution of Futures Trading.*

ment of contracts, although they have made forward contracts easier to use.[23]

Intermediary dealers have also attempted to reduce the default cost problem in forward contracts. Indeed, intermediary dealers (including commercial banks in the foreign currency area), in addition to reducing transaction costs, at times play an important risk-reduction role. In particular, they objectify, and thereby reduce, some of default risk cost by incorporating it in the bid-asked spread.

Futures markets. The illiquidity of forward contracts, together with expansion of demand for them, prompted the development of futures markets. When forward trading in an asset reaches a sufficiently large volume, it often becomes profitable to create a futures market. In this respect, many futures markets are applications of economies of scale to transactions in forward markets. The existence of forward markets and reasonably developed spot markets facilitated the establishment of futures markets. Most early futures markets were set up at exchanges for spot market transactions. Such exchanges were a natural location for the creation of a futures market inasmuch as potential transactors in futures and information relevant to futures were located there.

Speculative investors as well as commercial firms foster the emergence and efficiency of futures markets, and in turn the development of these markets facilitates speculative investment as well as hedging. In part, it is a pool of speculative money that creates the potential economies of scale that motivate the creation of a futures market. The mechanisms, low margin requirements and clearinghouse arrangements, that characterize such formally organized markets are

---

[23] Indeed, as Irwin points out,

"The prominence of rules providing for margin deposits suggests that difficulties with the fulfillment of time [or forward] contracts were not uncommon among the members of the various exchanges. Subsequent developments suggest that the adoption of such rules was none too effective in assuring the fulfillment of the contracts." (Irwin, *Evolution of Futures Trading*, pp. 35-36.)

The enforcement of forward contracts is burdened by the difficulty of securing redress in case of contractual default. If a contract is not fulfilled at maturity, the plaintiff has recourse only from the party with whom he or she negotiated, not from the party that may have been the source of the problem. The same is true for the defendant. Needless to say, this procedure is cumbersome at best, and is extremely costly, if not prohibitively so, in many cases.

The default cost problem for forward contracts is greater than that for loans (which embody one element of a forward transaction) because the former entails a two-way default risk problem, whereas the latter tends to entail only a one-way problem.

byproducts of the liquidity such markets offer and, in turn, contribute to still greater market liquidity.

There has been a tendency for futures contracts for related assets to be traded on the same futures exchange in much the same way that related spot assets tend to be traded on the same spot exchange. For example, futures for the different foreign currencies are traded on the same exchange (the International Money Market of the Chicago Mercantile Exchange). Of late, however, exchanges have begun to compete with one another by introducing their own futures contracts for assets traded elsewhere. Such competition has been especially intense in the new financial instrument futures. The proliferation of contracts on a given asset is likely to continue; it is also likely to prompt increasing regulatory concern about the effect on market liquidity. At present, there are eleven futures exchanges in the United States.[24]

Clearinghouses were established to assure the fulfillment of futures contracts. The clearinghouse interposes itself between all buyers and sellers of futures contracts—it takes the long (short) side of all short (long) positions of market participants. Thus, the financial resources of the clearinghouse assure the integrity of both sides to all futures contracts. Clearinghouse settlement procedures are economically feasible because of the standardization of futures contracts and the attendant large volume of futures transactions. Membership in a clearinghouse is open to any exchange member who can meet its requirements, including a deposit of money as a reserve against possible losses. To reduce their risks, clearinghouses require that both parties (exchange members) to a futures contract deposit cash margins (that is, a percentage of the value entailed in the transaction) with the clearinghouse. The size of these deposits must be adjusted to reflect changes in prevailing market prices of futures. Members of an exchange, in turn, collect cash (or cash equivalent) margins from their customers. The exchanges provide for the adjudication of disputes and imposition of penalties in situations of contract defaults.[25]

---

[24] Amex Commodity Exchange, Inc., Chicago Board of Trade, Chicago Mercantile Exchange and International Money Market, Commodity Exchange, Inc., Kansas City Board of Trade, Mid-America Commodity Exchange, Minneapolis Grain Exchange, New York Cocoa Exchange, New York Coffee and Sugar Exchange, New York Cotton Exchange and Associates, and New York Mercantile Exchange. As with individual futures markets, exchanges may come and go. The Pacific Commodities Exchange closed on May 10, 1976. For a listing of futures traded on each exchange, see Commodity Futures Trading Commission, *1977 Annual Report.*

[25] Cf. Irwin, *Evolution of Futures Trading,* pp. 40-41.

A futures market's organization makes it easier to ascertain the quality of a contract (both the quality of the asset for future delivery and the quality of the opposite party to the transaction) and reduces the cost of carrying a position in such a contract. The cost of ascertaining the quality of a contract is reduced through standardization of asset quality, centralization of transactions, open and competitive asking and bidding for transactions, and enforcement of contractual obligations. The cost of carrying a position in a contract is reduced through low margin requirements, enforcement of contractual obligations, and the standardization of asset quality.[26]

Reducing these costs increases the marketability of contracts and decreases uncertainty about the underlying value (price) of such contracts, thereby enhancing liquidity of the markets. These cost reductions also improve the efficiency with which futures prices estimate future spot prices.

Exchanges specify the terms and conditions of contracts. Contract terms and conditions that are consistent with commercial practices in spot markets encourage commercial use of futures markets. One of the most important terms is the quality or grade of an asset that is deliverable on a contract. Such specification helps to reduce uncertainty about the quality of the asset and thereby lowers the cost of acquiring information on the contract.[27] To help prevent cornering of markets, exchanges often specify a range of commodity qualities that may be delivered on a futures contract. Although the use of a range contributes to orderly market conditions, it also reduces information about asset quality. One important side effect of specifying a range, as opposed to a single grade, for delivery is the low volume with which futures are used for the taking of delivery; those holding long positions may not receive the grade that they desire, and thus seek to close out their positions prior to a contract's maturity.[28] The delivery provision does, however, assure the tendency of spot and futures prices to converge at the maturity of a contract.

---

[26] Low margin requirements, however, could contribute to trend movements in price and foster trend trading. For example, if large brokerage houses advise their speculative customers to take positions in relatively illiquid futures, and if stop loss orders of such customers are reasonably similar (as they tend to be), one set of stop loss orders—if activated—could trigger other sets. To the extent that this happens, the increase of a market's current liquidity could be offset (perhaps more than offset) by a decrease of market liquidity in the long run. This possible problem, which is not unique to futures markets, has not received sufficient attention.

[27] In making such specifications, exchanges often developed new and more detailed grades of commodities than had been in existence on spot exchanges.

[28] The low volume of deliveries is often exaggerated, however. Too often, data on the volume of deliveries are presented as a percentage of the volume of

Exchanges also specify those deliverable supplies that are deliverable at par, the discounts for nonpar deliveries, and the number and location of delivery points. In addition, they establish the number and location of certified warehouses for storage, the number and time of monthly maturity dates for a given contract designation, the volume of an asset per contract, and the magnitude of the margin requirement.

Just as futures contracts for some assets come and go, and just as the maturity limits of futures contracts for a given asset change over time, so changes may also occur in commercial practices in spot markets. Exchanges review the terms and conditions of contracts, so that changes in commercial practices may be reflected in new or revised terms and conditions. In order to facilitate and encourage commercial use of futures markets, the system of contract design should be sufficiently flexible to meet in a responsible way changes that occur in commercial practices.

The use of futures markets by commercial firms for hedging risk entails certain benefits and costs. Although the gross benefits of hedging through futures contracts are likely to be somewhat smaller than those gained through forward contracts, the costs of hedging through futures contracts are usually significantly lower. As a result, the commercial use of futures has been growing compared to forward contracts.

Hedging through futures rather than forward contracts has smaller gross benefits because of the greater standardization of futures contracts—with regard to quality of asset, volume of asset, contract maturity, and location of delivery. With such standardization, the futures price has a lower degree of covariation with the spot price of specific assets than does the forward price of tailor-made contracts.

Futures markets reduce all elements of hedging costs for commercial firms—the costs of effecting contracts and the costs of carrying positions in them. In some instances, the reduction of hedging costs is so large that firms which had used a tailor-made forward contract, or had not previously hedged at all, use a futures contract in an asset that differs from, but is related to, their spot asset ("cross hedging"). For example, soybean oil futures contracts sometimes

transactions in a given contract. Such ratios, which are typically quite low, may not indicate an appropriate relative magnitude of deliveries. Data on the volume of deliveries as a percentage of an average open interest on a contract (during a period near its maturity) would appear to represent more meaningful information. The latter ratios generally are considerably higher than the former. For example, for the 1974 corn crop, deliveries were less than 1 percent of the volume of transactions (23 billion bushels) whereas they averaged nearly 20 percent of the previous month-end open interest. See Commodity Futures Trading Commission, Office of Education, *Futures Information for Educators*, no. 8 (December 28, 1978).

are used to offset exposed positions in cottonseed oil, or Treasury bill futures are used to offset exposure in certificates of deposit, or corn futures are used to offset exposure in grain sorghum.

The premiums embedded in futures prices—an important element of hedgers' carrying costs—are usually lower than the premiums in forward prices that had existed. The reduction of these premiums reflects the increased willingness of speculators to assume open positions in contracts for future transactions, that in turn is attributable to their lower costs of effecting and carrying open positions in futures contracts. The reduction of speculators' carrying costs stems not only from lower default risk but also from the specialization of function and economies of scale in price forecasting that standardization of contract makes possible.

The increased willingness of hedgers and speculators to use markets for future transactions makes these markets both more liquid and more efficient, as activity of one group reinforces activity of the other. The greater market participation fosters better market information about future spot prices.

Over time, futures markets usually become more efficient than the corresponding spot markets. This development is somewhat paradoxical in view of the fact that futures markets enhance the efficiency of the corresponding spot markets. A principal factor contributing to the greater efficiency of futures markets is the greater ease with which futures may be carried. This explanation is also somewhat paradoxical, because futures markets tend to reduce the cost of carrying assets (holding inventories) in spot markets.

4
Option Markets

Options markets are special types of markets for future transactions. They are markets for contracts governing rights, but not obligations, of purchasers to future spot transactions.

The Development of Option Contracts

Option contracts provide a form of insurance against future contingencies. Conceivably, an option contract could be written to cover almost any type of future contingency. A common type of option contract is an agreement under which a lawyer provides a client with whatever services the client may need on a particular matter (or matters) during a specified period of time in exchange for a fee, or retainer.

Usually, option contracts will be written only on underlying assets for which quality and quantity can be specified precisely (as in the case of futures). The most common option contracts are for securities or commodities. Records of such contracts can be traced at least as far back as the seventeenth century. They were quite popular in the 1920s and early 1930s. Recently, there has been a renewed interest in them. Options on futures also exist, but are currently limited to London commodity exchanges which allow options, *inter alia,* on the cocoa, coffee, and sugar futures of the London markets.

In an option contract, the purchaser secures the right—but not the obligation—to buy (a call option) or sell (a put option) a specified quantity and quality of an asset (actual or futures) at a specified price (the "striking price"), either at a specified date or at any time over a specified period (whichever way the contract is written) in exchange for a present payment, or premium. The purchaser of these rights is sometimes referred to as the grantee; it is the grantor who issues, or sells, or grants the rights.

Options on securities and commodities could be written with regard to factors other than price level. Indeed it is possible to imagine an option being written against the difference between the highest and the lowest price of an asset during some period of time. The fact that option contracts are usually written in terms of a striking price likely reflects the economic demands of commercial purchasers of options.

Option contracts for an asset—put and/or call—probably develop in response to the economic demands of commercial firms and speculators (in futures as well as actuals) for insurance against major price movements of that asset. Commercial firms and speculative investors will seek to buy a put option for insurance against a major price decline; they will seek to buy a call option for insurance against a major price increase. For commercial firms, options reduce the risk of exposed positions (existing or anticipated) in actuals; for speculative investors, options reduce the speculative nature of their investments. Those seeking to purchase options also include speculators who hope to profit from favorable price movements in the underlying asset; their economic demands also contribute to the emergence of options.

An option contract will be written ("granted") only if it appears to be profitable to do so. For an option to be profitable, its premium —the price that buyers are willing to pay—must be sufficient to cover the cost (including a competitive rate of return) to the writer, or grantor, of the contract.

The grantor's costs include transaction costs of writing the option and the costs of carrying a position in it. The carrying costs include opportunity costs and, more importantly, the effective payments that must be made to the grantee (purchaser) if and when the latter decides to exercise the option (which, for most options, may occur at any time during the life of the option). Such effective payments consist of the difference between the amount that the grantor has to pay for acquiring the asset in the market (or, in case that the asset is already in the grantor's possession, its market value) less the amount that the grantor receives from the grantee, as stipulated in the contract (through the striking price). In addition, the grantor's costs include that of bearing the uncertainty about the probability and amount of such contingent payments. Thus, the grantor's costs depend, *inter alia*, on expectations (including the confidence attached thereto) of the probability and magnitude that the price of the underlying asset will be lower (higher) than the striking price of the put (call) option.

The magnitude of put and call premiums is a function, *inter alia*, of the expected price movement of the underlying asset (including the confidence attached thereto), of exposed positions in the underlying asset, of the attitudes of commercial firms and speculative investors to this exposure, and of the willingness of speculators and commercial firms to write options. The premium on put (call) contracts—for a specified maturity, and for a given differential between the market price and the striking price of the underlying asset—will usually vary directly with the writers' costs. Thus, as with premiums embedded in futures, option premiums are determined by demand and supply factors.

The commercial firms that write options usually have an offsetting exposed position (partial or total) in the spot market. For example, the commercial firm that writes a call option contract on copper may hold some inventory of copper. In such a situation, the option writing provides some expected premium income and, at the same time, tends to alter the firm's risk exposure and profit opportunity. In so doing, it may allow the firm to expand its operations.

Because commercial practices in spot markets are such that long exposure to price risk usually is greater than short exposure, the commercial demand to purchase put options is likely to be greater than that for call options. However, for the same reason, commercial willingness to write call options is likely to be greater than that for put options. Since speculators in actuals or futures also have (on balance) long exposure, they also will tend to have a preference for purchasing puts and writing calls. The asymmetry of commercial and speculative exposure to price risk thus tends to generate an asymmetry in the demand for and supply of option contracts. It is possible that this asymmetry is in part responsible for the greater open interest in calls than in puts; the cost of purchasing puts may become too high in relation to the premium income that firms may receive from issuing calls.

The size of the premium tends to vary directly with the expected probability that an option will be exercised. Thus, the premium is typically larger, the more favorable the relationship between the striking price and the current price of the asset, and the longer the period until contract maturity.[1] The holder of an option must pay a

---

[1] Henry Jarecki has indicated that the premium on a one-year option contract that is written at the market (that is, whose striking price is equal to the then-prevailing price of the underlying asset) typically lies between 5 and 15 percent of the

price for the privilege of having a longer period in which to exercise a contract. However, the difference in price, or premium, is usually less than proportionate to differences in the life of the contract. This is probably because near-term option contracts are subject to greater price variability than are distant-term ones, in much the same way that near-term futures prices tend to fluctuate more than distant-term ones.

Just as futures prices are not unbiased estimates of future spot prices, so option premiums are not actuarial estimates of expected market volatility. Such premiums, like those in futures, embody some compensation for the insurance services the option writers provide. Improvements in price information about the underlying asset will reduce option premiums, just as with futures. Also, however, uncertainty about governmental policy tends to weaken the efficiency of option markets, as with futures. Indeed, the cost of writing options may become larger, perhaps prohibitively so, for the more distant expiration dates, as prices become more difficult to predict. In this connection, it is worth noting that option premiums (as a percentage of striking prices) on several commodities have increased since the mid-1960s.[2]

Some recent data on call options for copper and Alcoa securities illustrate the point that premiums generally will be higher, the lower the striking price and the longer the time until contract maturity. These principles apply to put options as well. The striking price of a call (put) option in an asset may be above or below (below or above) the current, or spot, price of that asset. However, the striking price of a call (put) option plus the premium will be higher (lower) than the spot price. This difference is the implicit payment to the grantors, or writers, to protect them against possible losses in the insurance services that they provide. Table 1 illustrates this relationship.

In all cases, the striking price plus the premium are higher than the spot price of the underlying asset. For example, in the first quotation for copper (the March 1979 contract), the striking price of $.72 plus the premium of $.017 are $.052 greater than the spot price. This difference of $.052 is the implicit payment (or implicit premium) to writers of these call option contracts.

---

value of the underlying asset. Henry Jarecki, "The Birth of the Market," *Euromoney* (September 1978), pp. 141-42.

[2] See Bean, Bower and Co., "The Impact of Option Trading upon Futures Trading in the London Commodity Exchanges," a report submitted to the Commodity Futures Trading Commission by Bean, Bower and Co. of Manchester, England (July 1976).

TABLE 1

Closing Call Option Premiums for Copper and for Alcoa Shares, January 2, 1979

Underlying Asset	Striking Price	Contract Date (1979)				Spot Price
		January	March	April	July	
Copper commodity		dollars per pound				
(50,000 pounds)	.72		.017		.059	.685
	.76		.007		.040	.685
	.84		.001		.019	.685
Alcoa securities		dollars per share				
(100 shares)	45.00	2.75		4.63	6.00	47.00
	50.00	.38		1.88	3.50	47.00

Sources: Copper quotations computed from data of Metals Quality Corporation reported in *Journal of Commerce*, January 3, 1979. (Note that Metals Quality Corporation has a wider variety of call options than is reported in the *Journal of Commerce*.) Alcoa quotations are from *Wall Street Journal*, January 3, 1979.

Generally, the higher the striking price, the lower the potential gains of the writers (or the larger their costs). This is because the size of the premium limits the earnings of call option writers; and a lower premium goes with the higher striking price. To receive compensation for their worsened situation, call option writers will see to it that the increase of striking price for a given call option contract (including duration to maturity) will be greater than the reduction of premium—thus assuring themselves of larger implicit payments (or implicit premiums). A comparison, for example, of the different striking prices on the March 1979 call option contract on copper illustrates this point: the increase of striking price from $.72 to $.76 is associated with a reduction of premium from $.017 to $.007. In general, call option purchasers appear to be willing to pay larger premiums in exchange for lower striking prices (and lower implicit payments).

Although the premium often is regarded as the cost of insurance to the purchaser of a call option, it is only one of the two aspects of this cost. It represents the maximum possible cost of insurance; the implicit premium, the other aspect, represents the payment to call option writers that is designed to protect them against possible losses. These two aspects of insurance cost are inversely related. The fact that many combinations of the inverse relationship may exist simultaneously is attributable, *inter alia*, to different attitudes toward risk and different market expectations by purchasers and writers of call options.

As a transferable call option contract approaches maturity, the implicit premiums tend to approach zero. This is attributable to a reduction of the option writer's price uncertainty and opportunity costs. The explicit premiums tend to approach the excess of the underlying asset's price over the striking price as the expiration date approaches; where the underlying asset's price is less than the striking price, the probability becomes greater that the explicit premiums will be zero.

In practice, the implicit premium on an option contract should not be estimated on the basis of current spot price but on the basis of the spot price that is expected to exist in the contract's expiration month. The expected future spot price is, however, a subjective estimate. The forward or futures price—though a biased estimation itself because of premiums embedded in their price—could perhaps be used as a proxy for the expected future spot price in estimating the size of the implicit premium in an option contract. Thus, the implicit premiums on the March and July 1979 call options on copper could be adjusted by substituting the March and July 1979 futures prices of copper for the spot copper price. On January 2, 1979, the March price closed at about $.70 per pound and the July price, about $.73 per pound. The fact that these prices were higher than the Januray 2, 1979, spot price suggests that the implicit premiums are not as large as they at first appear.

The Development of Market Organization

Option contracts and markets are both prompted and facilitated by the development of efficient markets for actuals and futures; the development of efficient spot and futures markets fosters a commercial and speculative demand for options to reduce or alter exposed positions in these markets and provides to option markets useful information on already standardized underlying assets.

It is not surprising that the quantity and quality of an asset deliverable on an option contract usually are similar to those for delivery on the corresponding futures. For example, the size of the option contract (50,000 pounds) for the dealer options in copper is twice that of a futures contract on copper. It also is not surprising that the expiration dates of options typically are related to the expiration dates of the corresponding futures and that the maximum duration to maturity of options often is related to the maximum duration to maturity of the corresponding futures.

Option contracts on commodities may be written and purchased on London exchanges or through option dealers. Although London and dealer options tend to be of limited marketability (they may be assigned from one party to another), the planned exchange-traded options on commodities and futures in the United States should provide much greater marketability (contract positions would be alterable by offsetting transactions). In this respect, the planned exchange program will be similar to the exchange-traded stock options in the United States.

The efficiency of an option market is similar in many respects to that of a futures market. The option premium is, however, unique; its quality entails the accuracy with which it estimates the expected price movement—the probability and magnitude—of the underlying asset. The development of market organization is, in part, the development of option premiums as more accurate estimators of expected price movements. Dealers in options and, later, exchanges play an important role in reducing the premium and in making it a more objective indicator of expected price movement.

Option dealers tend to reduce the cost of option writing and thereby tend to reduce option premiums. Many dealers reduce their costs of writing options by taking a position (usually a partial position) in the underlying (or related) asset. For example, a writer of call options on copper may purchase physical copper or copper futures; a writer of put options on copper may sell copper futures. The amount of net copper holdings (actuals and futures) is likely to increase as the spot price of copper increases and to decrease as the spot price of copper decreases. Such purchases and sales, which may occur continually during the life of the option contract, entail transaction costs to option dealers. The dealers will incur such objective costs in order to reduce their subjective costs (risk); presumably, the reduction of subjective costs will be greater than the objective costs incurred. The premium income of option writing serves to offset (on balance) the dealers' costs (objective and subjective).

In effect, option dealers buy insurance (through the partial covering of their option writing) in order to provide insurance (that is, sell option contracts) to their customers in a more efficient way. Option dealers also reduce their costs by writing options at different striking prices; the diversification reduces their subjective costs (risk). With competition, the reduction of dealers' costs leads to lower option premiums.

The Role of Exchanges. Organized option markets, such as those operating through exchanges, come into existence because of expected economies of scale in the granting and purchase of options as well as in the trading of such options. In turn, such markets encourage the writing and purchase of option contracts as well as their trading. The markets tend to improve information by standardizing contract terms, and they mitigate default risk through the establishment of clearinghouses. The effects of organized option markets on direct users of option contracts are indeed much the same as those for futures.

The specification of contract terms by an exchange is an important ingredient of a viable exchange program of option writing and purchase. In particular, the exchange must determine not only which assets are appropriate for option contracts, but also the terms and conditions of such contracts, including the quantity and quality of the underlying asset, the striking prices, and expiration dates. As with futures, exchanges select terms and conditions of option contracts so as to promote their commercial usefulness. This means that some restrictions must exist on the variety of contracts on a given asset (such as with regard to striking prices and expiration dates), so as not to dilute liquidity.

The development of the organized markets for stock options illustrates some of the benefits of these markets and anticipates those from the planned exchange-traded option program for commodities and futures in the United States.

Prior to 1973, option contracts on equity securities were bought and sold in the over-the-counter market. Terms and conditions, such as striking prices and expiration dates, were not well standardized. The wide variety of option contracts that existed on a given equity security limited their liquidity.

Exchange-traded stock options were introduced in 1973 by the Chicago Board Options Exchange (CBOE). With this development came the standardization of contract terms and the establishment of a clearinghouse, the Options Clearing Corporation, which reduced default risk. For option contracts, the CBOE has chosen only security issues of large, well-capitalized firms with a large volume of shares outstanding.

The emergence of CBOE and the concomitant improvement in the quality of information have reduced substantially the bid-offer spreads on option quotations.[3] In addition, the volume of trans-

---

[3] See Securities and Exchange Commission, *Report of the Special Study of the Options Markets* (February 1979), ch. 1, p. 12.

actions and open interest in stock options have increased dramatically since 1973. In particular, transactions have increased

> . . . from under 6 million call option contracts in 1974 to almost 39 million contracts in the first nine months of 1978. When the CBOE first opened for business, it sponsored trading in call options on sixteen common stock issues. By the fall of 1978, four additional exchanges were sponsoring trading in options. . . . The five options exchanges presently sponsor trading in call options on about 220 stock issues and put options on twenty-five of those issues.[4]

The Choice among Options. A wide array of options on commodities and securities currently exists. Options on futures are at present quite limited. However, they are likely to grow when the pilot program of exchange-traded options begins in the United States. For assets in which options on both actuals and futures exist, those on futures may become the predominant hedging instrument among options.

Options on futures will be fostered by the high liquidity of futures markets. It is true that for firms seeking to hedge exposed positions in spot markets, options on futures are likely to provide somewhat smaller gross benefits than options on actuals. Options on futures will have a more distant relationship to the exposed position in the spot market than options on actuals. Thus, the direct covariation between the price of the hedged transaction and that of the exposed position—the proximate objective of hedging—is likely to be lower for options on futures than for options on actuals. However, the cost of hedging through options on futures is likely to be less than that through options on actuals, inasmuch as options on futures are likely to be more liquid than options on actuals. For speculative investors in futures, the benefits of hedging through options on futures are also greater than those of options on actuals.

The Choice of Hedging: Options vs. Futures

Commercial firms seeking to hedge exposed positions in actuals could choose either instrument—futures or options—assuming both were available. The availability of both is useful in that it gives commercial firms a wider range of choice.

In some respects, commercial firms seeking to hedge exposed positions in actuals obtain greater gross benefits through options

---

[4] Kenneth D. Garbade and Monica M. Kaicher, "Exchange-Traded Options on Common Stock," Federal Reserve Bank of New York, *Quarterly Review*, vol. 3, no. 4 (Winter 1978-79), p. 26.

than through futures. Both are designed to reduce the risk of exposure (actual or expected). Options provide one-way insurance, so that the commercial firm may gain from movements of price in the direction opposite to that insured against. In contrast, futures provide two-way insurance, so there may be no gains from movements in the price level. In addition, the benefits of futures are constrained by uncertainty attached to the prospective maturity structure of prices (the bases).

The cost of hedging through futures and options also differs. Transaction costs exist for both. In the case of options, the maximum insurance cost (the premium) is known in advance, and is constant for the duration of a given contract.[5] For futures, the maximum insurance cost is not known in advance because the premiums embedded in futures prices (a principal component of the insurance cost) depend on uncertain expectations with regard to future spot prices, and hence are uncertain. However, for many futures, especially those characterized by strong hedging interests on both sides of the market, such costs are likely to be less than the cost of options. The lower hedging costs through futures may enable futures to remain the predominant hedging instrument.

The choice of hedging instrument is affected by a number of factors. One is the firm's judgment about the market's assessment of option premiums and the implicit payments to option writers as well as of premiums embedded in futures prices. To the extent that a firm's expectations, of either type, differ from those of the market, its cost or benefit of hedging, in one or both types, will be affected. For example, a firm would not purchase an option unless the expected price movement of the underlying asset were such that an unfavorable price change could be larger than the premium. A second factor affecting a firm's choice of hedging instrument is its attitude toward risk. The greater its aversion to risk, the greater the likelihood that it would choose options, particularly those involving small premiums.

It is interesting to note a similarity between the risk-reducing role of futures and options. Futures reduce the risk of two entities (firms with exposure in actuals and options) through the assumption of a new form of risk by another entity (speculators with open positions in futures). Options reduce the risk of two entities (firms with exposed positions in actuals and futures) through the assumption of a new form of risk by another entity (a writer of naked, or uncovered,

---

[5] For transferable options, any favorable change in the premium may be viewed as a reflection of developments (actual or anticipated) associated with the benefits of the one-way insurance.

options) or through a change in risk exposure by another entity (an option writer who holds a position in the underlying or related asset).

The speculator in options is likely to be a different type of individual or firm than the speculator in futures. In particular, the successful speculator in options is likely to have a comparative advantage in predicting relatively large price movements; whereas the successful speculator in futures is likely to have a comparative advantage in predicting relatively small price movements. Because the nature of expertise in the two markets differs, the money devoted to speculative investment in options may well come from previously unsuccessful speculators in futures (because the nature of these markets did not complement their particular expertise) or from elsewhere in the economy.

5
Benefits of Improving Market Efficiency

Establishing a new market or enhancing the efficiency of an existing one brings both direct and indirect economic benefits. The direct benefits derive from the ability to carry out transactions more efficiently; the indirect benefits derive from more efficient collection and dissemination of information on the terms of transactions.

In the rudimentary stage of a market's development, the principal benefits are direct ones; but in the more advanced stages of development, the indirect benefits are of greater significance than the direct ones. Indeed, well-functioning markets in an advanced free enterprise economy have benefits that extend far beyond those realized by direct users of the markets. And, yet, the indirect benefits of market development have received little attention.

Just as well-functioning markets in an advanced free enterprise economy have pervasive beneficial effects, so any malfunctioning of such markets may have deleterious effects that extend far beyond those to direct users. For this reason, the orderly functioning of markets, though important in its own right, becomes crucial as the degree of development of an economy and its markets advances. It is in this area—the orderly functioning of markets—that regulation plays its principal role.

The transactors in a market are the proximate contributors to a market's establishment and organization. That role is not surprising in view of the benefits that the transactors realize. However, all users of the market—indirect as well as direct—benefit from the improvement of information, as do all users of related markets. In addition, an increase in one market's efficiency encourages its use, and that of related markets, by new as well as existing users; and this expansion of use compounds the economic benefits of market development. The beneficial effects of market development tend to become cumulative, as the level of such development advances; this is attributable to the greater variety and efficiency of related markets.

Ultimately, market development enhances the efficiency with which resources are allocated. Such development often allows the realization of economies of scale and attendant functional specialization in many aspects of production, marketing, and distribution of commodities and securities. In any case, it permits a given volume of resources to generate a larger output of consumer goods and services and to do so at lower prices.

The primary focus of this chapter is on the indirect benefits of improvements in spot, futures, and option markets. The direct benefits of market development have already been examined in earlier discussions of factors affecting the development of markets. It is, however, important to recognize that the direct and indirect benefits of market development are interrelated. The separate discussions are for analytical convenience only.

Spot Markets

Direct Benefits. Enhancement of a spot market's efficiency (especially its liquidity) reduces in two ways the transaction costs of those dealing in the asset. First, the diminished uncertainty about asset prices (underlying values) reduces search costs. Second, the enhanced marketability of assets lowers transfer costs (brokerage costs and a fraction of the bid-asked spread).

The reduction of transaction costs per unit of an asset facilitates the operations of all entities dealing in the asset. The increased ease of effecting transactions is likely to generate, *inter alia,* an increase in the volume of transactions in the asset and thereby still greater liquidity.

The increase of market liquidity serves to make a market more perfect in the Marshallian sense: the more certain an asset's underlying value and the greater its marketability, the more likely it will be that a single price will prevail for the same type of transaction (abstracting from transportation costs).[1] Greater uniformity of price fosters a more efficient set of transactions, thereby improving the allocation of resources.

Indirect Benefits. The improvement of market efficiency for an existing asset (real or financial) also has a wide array of indirect effects—

---

[1] See Alfred Marshall, *Principles of Economics*, Ninth Edition (New York: Macmillan Co., 1961), vol. 1, bk. 5, ch. 1.

on the market itself, on related markets, and on the interrelationship among the related markets.

Effects on the immediate market. The enhanced liquidity of an asset (especially the increased confidence attached to expectations about an asset's underlying value) may facilitate the decision making, including planning and pricing, of firms that produce or use that asset. For real assets, such as commodities, greater market liquidity may help firms reach decisions about production (output, distribution, and processing), marketing, or final use of a commodity. The decision-making process is likely to improve the most in the early stages of production (output and distribution), inasmuch as the standardization of asset quality, and thereby the potential for market development, is easiest there. For financial assets, such as securities, the greater market liquidity may help firms reach decisions about issuing new securities, trading existing securities, and processing or transforming existing securities through financial intermediation.

Improved decision making can increase efficiency in the production, marketing, or use of an asset (real or financial). In a competitive market structure, greater efficiency will tend to be reflected in more output of commodities or securities, together with lower prices or interest rates.[2]

Effects on related markets. The improvement of a given market's liquidity also enhances the liquidity of related markets, such as those for substitutes or complements. For example, improving the liquidity of a given market (say, the gold market)—such as reducing uncertainty about the price of an asset (gold)—conveys better information to the market for a related asset (say, silver); and this, in turn, reduces uncertainty about the price of the related asset (silver) and thereby enhances liquidity of the related market (the silver market). The increased liquidity of related markets facilitates their direct and indirect use, which has repercussive beneficial effects on outputs and prices of the related assets.

A wide array of markets may be related: markets for new assets at different geographical locations, for corresponding existing assets at different locations, for existing assets at different trading dates (spot and future), for complementary assets (new and existing, in different locations, on different trading dates), and for substitute assets (new and existing, in different locations, on different trading dates). As a

---

[2] Alfred Marshall referred to the benefits of such a development as an increase of "consumers' surplus." *Principles of Economics,* vol. 1, bk. 3, ch. 6, and bk. 5, chs. 13 and 14. Also, see John R. Hicks, "The Rehabilitation of Consumers' Surplus," *The Review of Economic Studies,* vol. 9 (1941), pp. 108–16.

result, an increase in the liquidity of any one market may induce extensive economic benefits throughout the array of related markets.

Several of these market relationships are especially important. For example, greater liquidity in existing commodity and securities markets improves the working of markets for new output and new security issues,[3] fosters the emergence and development of futures and option markets, and enhances the working of markets for the same asset at different trading centers.

In addition, greater liquidity of existing commodity markets improves the working of securities markets for those companies that produce or use the commodities in question. For example, better information about the price of a commodity (say, wheat) improves the working of markets for new securities issued by companies that deal in wheat.

Effect on market relationships. The enhanced efficiency of a given market not only improves the efficiency of related markets; it also integrates better the wide array of related markets (with it and with one another). As each of the assets becomes more marketable, their markets become more closely related. Thus, we can expect to see a closer integration of any given asset's production and use, a closer integration of different trading dates of a given asset, a closer integration of different regional markets for a given asset, and a closer integration of securities and commodity markets.[4]

Implications of closer market integration. As a result of the increased integration of markets, more and better information is brought to bear on individual markets, and prices become more closely attuned to market forces. This improves the allocation of resources.

The development of more and better information also imparts greater objectivity to market differentials. As a result, the risk premiums attaching to low-grade commodities and securities become smaller, and the liquidity advantages of standardization become

---

[3] Cf. Frederick Lavington, *The English Capital Market* (London: Methuen and Co., Ltd., 1921).

[4] It may be useful to note that the differences between securities and commodity markets are not as sharp as they may at first glance appear: the financing and real output of business firms are inherently interrelated. Any improvement in the financing opportunities of a business enterprise (possibly induced by improvements in securities markets) has repercussive beneficial effects on the real output of a business firm (including the possibility that improvements may be induced in commodity markets through the application of economies of scale). Similarly, any improvement in the real output opportunities of a business firm (possibly induced by improvements in commodity markets) has repercussive beneficial effects on the financing of a business firm (including the possibility that improvements may be induced in securities markets through the application of economies of scale).

smaller. This development, which probably appears only at an advanced stage of market development, is important. With a reduction of uncertainty, price differences for a given asset will better reflect differences in quality.[5]

The increased efficiency of markets and their attendant closer integration may well mean that prices will tend to be more variable on a day-to-day basis. However, this effect will be counterbalanced by a reduction of price fluctuations over the long run. Adjustments to demand-supply conditions will be quicker and continuous, rather than being postponed until a disequilibrium becomes recognized, with resultant large and discrete price changes.[6] Smaller long-run price fluctuations reduce the uncertainty attaching to prices in the distant future, and thereby promote greater output, particularly of a long-term investment nature. This effect may be of considerable importance to the long-run growth of an economy.

Furthermore, and of significance, the enhanced market efficiency of related markets and their increased integration foster competitive market conditions. The cost of information to market participants (actual and prospective) is reduced, and it thus becomes unlikely that one or a few firms could dominate (actually or potentially) market information (and thereby the market). To the extent that market conditions become more competitive, the allocation of resources improves.

Other observations. Three final observations are in order. First, the induced improvements in related markets have reciprocal beneficial effects on the original market. Thus, the ultimate improvement in the original market's liquidity is greater than at first may be apparent. Improvements in related markets are similarly augmented.

Second, the improvement of a market's liquidity is likely to strengthen the forces originally responsible for its liquidity. Thus, an enhancement of market liquidity is likely to foster standardization of the underlying asset, and improvements in its storage capability and its transportation technology. The increased benefits that now accrue to such improvements tend to stimulate them.[7] And any such improvements will make the market even more liquid.

---

[5] It is interesting to observe that the primary function of spot exchanges at an advanced stage of market development (that is, decentralized spot markets) may well be the collection and dissemination of information on quality differentials in spot prices.

[6] Cf. Milton Friedman, "The Case for Flexible Exchange Rates," in idem, *Essays in Positive Economics* (Chicago: University of Chicago Press, 1953).

[7] In this connection, Charles Schultze has stated, "Most analyses of the nature of inventions suggest that they tended to occur in very rough conformity with eco-

In general, the recognition that liquid markets are beneficial stimulates developments that are conducive to market liquidity. Thus, the prospective benefits of greater market liquidity partly occasioned better information services about asset quality, including centralization of spot markets, commodity standardization, investments by security issuers in name recognition, and improvements in intermediation, in communication, and in the definition and enforcement of property rights. The prospective benefits of greater market liquidity also partly induced reductions in the cost of holding inventories, including improvements in markets for future transactions, in insurance services, in financing services, and in storage facilities.

Third, improvements in market efficiency are also likely to improve information in the nonmarket arena by providing a benchmark, or frame of reference, thereby facilitating nonmarket transactions. Indeed, market transactions are a complement to, as well as a substitute for, nonmarket ones. Improvements in a given market's efficiency may be expected to increase total transactions (off-market as well as market). Although it is not entirely clear whether the percentage of transactions through the market will increase, the improvement of information in the nonmarket arena may, over time, lead to the emergence of new markets. In the meantime, the improvement of such information may still have pervasive beneficial effects on firms' transactions and plans.

Forward and Futures Markets

The economic benefits of improving forward and futures markets— establishing new markets and enhancing the efficiency of already existing ones—are similar in many respects to those for spot markets. However, forward and futures have certain aspects—particularly, their multidimensional nature—that deserve special attention. In this connection, the added dimension of these markets' efficiency—the quality of information about future spot prices—is of special significance. The greater the efficiency of markets for future transactions, the more efficient is the forward or futures price as an estimator of expected future spot prices.

nomic needs and scarcities as signalled by prices and profitability." Charles Schultze, *The Public Use of Private Interest* (Washington, D.C.: The Brookings Institution, 1977), pp. 25-26. References are made to Jacob Schmooker, *Inventions and Economic Growth* (Cambridge, Mass.: Harvard University Press, 1966), and Vernon W. Ruttan, "Research on the Economics of Technological Change in American Agriculture," *Journal of Farm Economics*, vol. 42 (November 1960), pp. 735-54.

Direct Benefits. Enhancing the efficiency of markets for future transactions has an impact on the commercial firms and speculators who are direct users of these markets. For commercial firms, a more efficient market reduces the cost of hedging and thereby promotes this use of the markets. Lower hedging costs foster the expansion of output and facilitate the carrying of inventories; and this tends to promote functional specialization and attendant economies of scale in such activities.

For speculators, more efficient markets reduce the cost of speculation, and thereby encourage speculative activity in them. Added market participation by either commercial users or speculators increases market liquidity (and, more broadly, efficiency), thereby facilitating the markets' use by both groups.

Enhancing the efficiency of markets for future transactions also makes it easier to carry out purchases and sales of spot assets. This effect has received little attention, but it may be important (at least for a period of time) in some spot markets that are relatively illiquid. In such markets, large purchases and sales may cause wide price movements, which might be avoided by using futures markets. For example, a bank seeking to issue a large volume of certificates of deposit (CDs) of a certain maturity may feel that the volume of the issue is such and/or the liquidity of the market is such as to affect adversely the market price of its issue. In the past, such adverse price effects have induced banks to stretch out their issues over a period of time, even if they expected higher interest rates. If, however, a bank had such expectations about interest rates, it would wish to increase its liabilities as soon as possible. The emergence of futures markets in Treasury bills has enabled banks to expedite the increase in liabilities. Now, the bank can stretch out its sale of CDs by taking initially a short position in Treasury bill futures and then unwinding this position gradually over time, in accordance with the volume and dates of its CD issues.

In this example, the use of Treasury bill futures reduces the cost to a bank of issuing a large volume of liabilities at one time in an illiquid market. The use of Treasury bill futures is not, however, without its own cost. Transaction costs exist, and the price of such futures may not move in perfect unison with the price of Treasury bills, let alone CDs.[8]

---

[8] The price of commercial paper futures is likely to move in closer alignment with that of CDs than do the Treasury bill futures. However, the commercial paper futures have some liquidity problems of their own, and do not appear to be a useful instrument for mitigating the liquidity problems in the CD market.

Indirect Benefits. A more efficient market for future transactions in a given asset has indirect consequences for the market in question, for related markets, and for the interrelationship of the related markets (with the market in question and with one another).

Effects on immediate market. Reduced uncertainty about an asset's current forward or futures price, and especially the improved expectations about its future spot price, will help the commercial firms that produce or use this and related assets make planning and pricing decisions.[9] Better decision making tends to result in more output and lower prices.

Effects on related markets as a whole. Improving the efficiency of a market for future transactions tends to make related markets more efficient by conveying more and better information to these markets. The increased efficiency of related markets promotes their use, which usually has beneficial effects on the production and prices of the related assets.

A market for future transactions in a particular asset (say, a futures market for gold) has many related markets: spot, forward, and option markets for the underlying asset (gold); a similar set of markets, as well as futures, for assets bearing a complementary or substitutive relationship to the underlying asset; and in many of these markets a number of geographical trading centers. The spot markets include the markets for the new assets (newly produced or newly issued) as well as the existing assets; and the forward, futures, and option markets may embrace many different maturity dates of the assets (and, in the case of options, different striking prices).

The greater the number and variety of related markets, the larger the induced effects of better efficiency are likely to be. That is why market development in an advanced economy may have immense economic benefits. Because a futures market generally comes into existence at a stage of economic development when a wide array of markets is already functioning, its emergence is likely to generate pronounced beneficial effects.

Effects on spot markets. Markets for future and spot transactions in the same asset inherently are closely related, and an induced increase in a spot market's efficiency is likely to be pronounced.[10] In

---

[9] Futures markets usually provide more and better information than price forecasts at a given instant of time. Indeed, price forecasts are for practical purposes out of date, and therefore potentially misleading, when they are read and heard. Unfortunately, forecasters seldom issue a caveat to this effect.

[10] This inherent interrelationship of the efficiency of markets for spot and future transactions is very important, but has not, so far as I am aware, received much attention. In part, this lack of attention may be attributed to the focus of atten-

particular, information about current conditions in spot markets will be improved not only by better information about future spot prices, but also by the larger output and inventory holdings that more efficient hedging mechanisms encourage.

The induced increase in a spot market's efficiency is likely to take a number of forms. First of all, the development of a futures market is likely to reduce spreads in bid-asked price quotations for spot transactions. Evidence on changes in such spreads for Government National Mortgage Association (GNMA) securities after the emergence of a futures market for GNMA securities lends support to this point. In the last two months of 1975, shortly after the introduction of the GNMA futures contract (October 1975), the spread between bid and asked prices on 8-percent GNMAs was about 24/32nds of a point. In January 1976, the spread narrowed to about 20/32nds of a point, and by the spring of 1976, it had narrowed to about 16/32nds; in December 1976, the spread was even smaller (about 8/32nds). Since then, it has fluctuated between 8/32nds and 16/32nds of a point.

Part of the 1976 reduction in the bid-asked price spread on GNMA securities may have been due to a reduction of uncertainty about underlying economic conditions; part of the reduction may have come from innovations in the dealers' market; but part probably was caused by the introduction of the futures contract. The fact that bid-asked spreads on related securities, such as Federal National Mortgage Association securities and Treasury bonds, narrowed little (if any) during the 1976 period lends support to the idea that a futures market reduces bid-asked price spreads in spot markets.[11]

Secondly, the improvement of a market for future transactions may bring the different trading centers of a spot market into closer alignment. A futures market, with its open, competitive, and well-disseminated prices, often serves as a catalyst or basis for pricing transactions in spot markets. Indeed, more and more companies (such as dealers in the staple grains) are using near-term futures prices (often in a rather mechanical manner) to set prices for spot transactions, and this acts to reduce differences in prices for similar spot transactions at a given point in time. The greater uniformity of prices tends to occur at a given location as well as between locations. A recent study of regional differences in mortgage rates before and after

---

tion on the inherent interrelationship of spot and futures prices. This latter interrelationship is but one aspect of the more general interrelationship of these markets.

[11] It should also be recognized that the reduction of bid-asked spreads in GNMAs may contribute to a reduction of such spreads in related securities.

the introduction of the GNMA futures contract lends support to this point.[12]

Regional differences in price levels (and bases) are thus likely to reflect more accurately differences among regions in demand-supply conditions and in transportation costs. In Alfred Marshall's terminology, such spot markets are becoming more "perfect."[13]

Thirdly, greater efficiency in markets for future transactions has encouraged a decentralized system of spot markets, and this system reflects demand-supply conditions in a more accurate way than previously. For many assets traded on spot exchanges, days often pass with few or no transactions. Prices of near-term futures can often give a better indication of conditions in such spot markets than the somewhat arbitrary price quotations of an exchange committee. The emergence of futures markets has probably reduced the role of central, or terminal, spot markets in providing information about price levels. In fact, the development of futures markets has been accompanied by a decline in the use of price level quotations at spot exchanges. The principal informational role of central spot markets now appears to relate to discounts and premiums on quality differentials of transactions rather than to price levels (or bases).

As the importance of spot exchanges' price level information has dwindled, the proportion of spot transactions carried out on exchanges has declined. In addition, spot transactions as a whole (that is, off as well as on exchanges) appear to be a declining fraction of "cash transactions" (that is, of spot, forward, or futures transactions which result in delivery of an asset or service). In this connection, the development of futures markets has increased the direct use of "to arrive" contracts (that is, forward contracts maturing within thirty days) in relation to that of spot transactions, inasmuch as the "to arrive" market lies closer to the near-term futures market and thus can benefit more from the latter's development than can spot markets. In short, the nature of cash market transactions as well as sources of information about such transactions have been changing in response to market forces.[14]

---

[12] William P. Culbertson, Jr., "GNMA Futures Trading: Its Impact on the Residential Mortgage Market," unpublished paper (1977).

[13] Marshall, *Principles of Economics*, vol. 1, bk. 5, ch. 1.

[14] The changes in the mainstream of cash market transactions were noted by Commissioner Read Dunn at the public hearings (Winter 1977) held in connection with the Commodity Futures Trading Commission's review of spot price committees and in his paper, "Pricing Problems in the Food Industry," presented at the North Central Regional Conference on Pricing Problems in the Food Industry (with Emphasis on Thin Markets), Commodity Futures Trading Commission, Washington, D.C., March 2, 1978.

Under the new, decentralized system of spot markets, the day-to-day variation in the level of spot prices and in regional price differentials is likely to be greater than before. This increased price variability might suggest—at first glance—that uncertainty about conditions in spot markets was greater, and that such markets' efficiency was thus impaired. Such an interpretation, however, does not appear to be correct. Information flowing to spot markets has improved under the decentralized spot market system, and prices accordingly reflect more promptly changes that occur in demand-supply conditions. A lack of information leads to price inflexibility; such inflexibility prevents the immediate and continuing adjustment of resources in response to changes in demand-supply conditions in the market, and necessitates eventual larger price and resource adjustments.

Quicker and more continuous economic adjustments, with their smaller long-run price changes and smaller distant-term uncertainty, improve the allocation of resources. In particular, output, especially of a long-term investment nature, increases when there is less distant-term price uncertainty. This effect is fundamental to the growth and development of an economy.

The effect of futures markets on price variability has been the subject of many empirical studies. Most of them tend to show that futures markets reduce price variability, although few (if any) of them distinguish between near-term and distant-term price variability.[15]

Effect on competition. The development of futures markets is likely to increase competition in spot markets by reducing the cost of information to participants in such markets. A high cost of ascertaining information can be a barrier to new entrants into a field as well as to competition between large entities on one side of a market and small entities on the other. An efficient price information system tends to reduce this barrier to entry as well as to equalize the competitive strength of entities on different sides of a market.[16] In turn, more competitive conditions are likely to enhance the efficiency of spot markets.

[15] The studies that analyze price variability before and after a period of futures trading are probably the most informative. Such comparisons can be made when the government prohibits trading of futures in certain markets—such as onion futures in the United States—after the markets had been in existence. The case of onions is reviewed in Holbrook Working, "Futures Markets under Renewed Attack," *Food Research Institute Studies*, vol. 4, no. 1 (1963). Also, see B. A. Goss and B. S. Yamey, "Introduction: The Economics of Futures Trading," in B. A. Goss and B. S. Yamey, eds., *The Economics of Futures Trading* (New York: Halstead Press, 1976), pp. 36-37.

[16] The customary opposition to new futures markets by producers and large dealers is consistent with this possible effect.

The futures markets for copper did in fact help to dismantle the fixprice (producers') market for spot copper transactions—thereby helping to bring about more competitive copper prices. Kennecott, the largest U.S. copper producer, started the new system of pricing spot copper transactions directly off of near-term futures prices in June 1978. Subsequently, several other copper companies adopted similar pricing methods. This new system of spot prices culminated a development that had been under way for some time in the copper industry; producers' control over prices had been rather steadily declining during the past few years. Paradoxically, the new pricing system may help copper producers in ways that have not yet been widely recognized outside the industry. It may defuse governmental concerns about copper price increases during periods of moral suasion and may help to preclude governmental interference in copper during periods of price control.

Effects on forward markets. The development of futures markets may also strengthen forward markets. True, many transactions that had been carried out on forward markets will now be done on futures markets. However, futures markets have a complementary relationship as well as a substitutive one with forward markets. Indeed, the pricing mechanism of forward markets is likely to work better because of the new and improved information that futures markets provide. Just as prices in spot markets tend to be tied to near-term futures prices, so prices in forward markets tend to be tied to prices of their counterparts in futures markets. In fact, arbitrage transactions will tend to prevent forward prices from getting out of line with price developments in futures markets. The improved pricing mechanism of forward markets will encourage forward transactions: firms that previously had not used forward (or futures) markets may now do so, both as a hedge against exposed positions in spot markets and as a substitute for spot transactions.

The development of futures markets also is likely to mold commercial practices in spot and forward markets. Just as futures markets grow out of spot and forward markets and adopt many of their commercial practices, the development of futures markets, in turn, molds the development of spot and forward markets. For example, in order to realize more fully the benefits from improved information on future spot prices, spot and forward market transactions are likely to take on more and more of the standardized aspects of futures contracts. In fact, some changes in commercial practices in a spot or forward market may be motivated by the expectation that they will induce the formation or improvement of a futures market, and that such development in turn will favor the spot or forward market.

It is interesting to note that the introduction in 1970 of standardization in the mortgage field—the GNMA modified pass-through certificates—was followed rather quickly by the emergence in 1975 of the GNMA futures market. To be sure, the GNMA certificates were introduced for a different purpose—to bolster the housing industry by stimulating investment in mortgages. The certificates enable investors to purchase shares in a pool of FHA/VA insured mortgages, whose interest payments and repayment of principal are insured by GNMA; this insurance reduces uncertainty about the quality of mortgages, and thereby fosters investor demand. In addition to their original purpose, the standardized GNMA certificates allowed first a forward market and then a futures market in GNMAs to develop. This experience may well provide a useful lesson to participants in other markets.

Effects of recent innovations. The recently established futures for financial instruments and foreign currencies will probably generate, over time, the most pronounced benefits of futures markets. For these futures, the effects (direct and indirect) are the same as those for other futures. However, the underlying spot markets in these cases are more important than other spot markets: interest rates affect virtually every firm in the country, while exchange rates affect every multinational firm and many domestic firms.

Although the prices of securities and foreign exchange are likely to fluctuate more on a day-to-day basis, their greater long-run stability is of particular importance. Greater long-run stability of interest and foreign exchange rates will enable governments to reduce their intervention—that is typically designed to prevent disorderly markets but which in fact may well create such disorder—with beneficial effects on the efficiency of spot and futures markets.

The recent establishment of futures markets for debt securities will also tend to reduce the costs of some lenders and dealers (including mortgage bankers and securities dealers) in the money and capital markets. Similarly, the recent establishment of futures markets for foreign exchange will tend to reduce the cost incurred by some firms in hedging foreign exchange risk. These new futures markets are growing rapidly (in the types and volume of use), and in time may have a significant effect on the overall performance of our national economy.

In addition, the development of these futures markets will improve information on future interest and exchange rates, and this should be of value to government officials in their formulation and implementation of macroeconomic policy.[17] It is, however, important to recognize that the improvement in future price information reduces, but does not eliminate, the premiums embedded in forward and futures prices; these premiums render forward and futures prices biased estimators of future spot prices.

If governmental officials have different evaluations of the prospective course of interest and currency rates than the market appears to suggest, they should explore the reasons for such differences.[18] If the differences are attributable to inside infomation (for example, if the government is planning to undertake a different policy than that envisaged by the market), the government might do well to inform the public promptly. In this way, the market participants will not be misled and will gain confidence in spot and futures markets as conveyors of information, which will foster the efficiency of these markets.

It is, however, also important that governmental policy be flexible; policy adjustments are needed from time to time. For this reason, the government might do well to make known to the public the broad basis for its policy decisions so that the market can predict better what governmental policy may in fact be. This also will strengthen the markets' efficiency, and the government will be one of the principal beneficiaries of this improvement.

Final observation. The improvement of markets for future transactions tends to clarify price expectations, not only for transactions and decision making in the given and related markets (including interpolative maturities) but also for transactions and decision making in the nonmarket arena—maturities beyond the most distant-term ones of existing markets as well as for assets which do not at present have

---

[17] As with markets for other financial instruments, the emergence of futures markets for Treasury securities is likely to generate better future price information. The improvement is likely to occur for all maturities outstanding. However, the way in which such improvement occurs is likely to differ for different contract maturities. For shorter-term maturities, the futures rates are likely to be better estimators of future spot interest rates than are the implicit forward rates in the term structure of interest rates, because of the lower transaction costs of futures; for longer-term maturities, the implicit forward rates are likely to be the better estimators, inasmuch as some (albeit small) default risk exists on Treasury futures, but no such risk exists in the implicit forward rates. (See Richard W. Lang and Robert H. Rasche, "A Comparison of Yields on Futures Contracts and Implied Forward Rates," Federal Reserve Bank of St. Louis, *Review*, December 1978.) Even on the longer-term maturities, however, the development of the futures market for Treasury securities is likely to improve the efficiency of the implicit forward market, thereby improving information about interest rates in the future.

[18] See William Poole, "Using T-Bill Futures to Gauge Interest Rate Expectations," Federal Reserve Bank of San Francisco, *Economic Review*, Spring 1978.

markets. The improvement of price expectations about nonmarket phenomena may, over time, lead to the emergence of new markets. In the meantime, the improvement of such expectations—particularly, about distant-term future spot prices—may still have wide-ranging effects on firms' decision making, including the negotiation of contracts for future transactions and the improvement of long-term planning. Such effects—especially for debt securities and foreign exchange—may be of some importance to the development of our economy.

Option Markets

The benefits (direct and indirect) of option contracts and the markets on which they are traded parallel those of spot, forward, and futures markets. They directly benefit commercial firms and speculative investors who use such contracts to reduce or alter the risk of exposed positions in actuals or futures. The indirect benefit is the economic value of the information generated by option premiums.

The type of information generated by option premiums depends on the type of option contract considered—whether it be a put or a call. The variety of put and call options (for different maturities or striking prices) on the same asset improves information about the market's expectation, including the degree of symmetry, of price changes—both the probability and magnitude—for that asset.

Effects on Price Expectations. The information generated by option premiums helps the decision making of commercial firms who produce the underlying asset and both commercial firms and speculative investors who use it. In particular, option premiums impart information about expected price movements of the underlying asset (including the confidence attaching thereto), thereby aiding participants in the spot and futures markets.

The higher the call (put) premium on an asset (for a given asset price, striking price, and time to maturity), the greater the magnitude by which the price of the underlying asset may be expected to be above (below) the striking price during the period in question, and/or the greater the confidence attached to such an expectation. Such information is likely to affect expectations about future price levels and the confidence with which they are held. As a result, current spot and futures prices will likely be affected, as will premiums embedded in forward and futures prices. The adjustment of spot and futures prices to this new information about expected market conditions fosters better decisions by commercial firms and speculative investors.

New market information may well be revealed first in option markets. The rate of return to speculative investors with new information is likely to be greatest in option markets, in view of the high leverage of option contracts; so, option premiums may well be the first indicators of changes in market conditions. This early indication of market changes may expedite the adjustment of spot and futures prices—with beneficial effects on resource allocation—in much the same way that futures prices expedite the adjustment of spot prices. The greater short-run variability of spot and futures prices will be compensated by smaller long-run variability.

Effects on Market Efficiency. Also, and of significance, the new information that options provide about price expectations is likely to improve the efficiency of spot or futures markets for the underlying asset and the efficiency of related markets—in much the same way that futures improve the efficiency of markets for the underlying and related assets. In so doing, options bring the market for the underlying asset into closer contact with those for related assets. The increased efficiency of the related markets and their closer integration facilitate the use—direct and indirect—of these markets.

Arbitrageurs take positions such that prices in related markets (actuals, futures, options on actuals, and options on futures) approximately reflect the inherent economic interrelationship of the assets. The greater the efficiency of the related markets and the greater their integration, the easier it is for arbitrage to adjust the structure of market prices along patterns that represent inherent economic interrelationships.

Effects on Risk Assessment. Because of the premiums embedded in futures prices, commercial firms are not able to determine from a futures price what in fact the future spot price is expected to be. Premiums on options, however, may convey information about these price expectations. Indeed, premiums on options and the premiums embedded in futures are inextricably interrelated. More precisely, the risk elements in the carrying costs of option writers and of speculators in futures are inherently interrelated. For this reason, objective (public or market) information about option premiums provides information about the subjective premiums in futures.

Premiums on futures are heavily influenced by the risk component of speculators' carrying costs, which is the principal element of speculators' costs (carrying costs and transaction costs). The magnitude of the risk cost, and thereby the speculators' total cost, is necessarily a subjective estimate by the different market participants. These estimates will differ with differences in expectations about a future spot price as well as with differences in the degree of confidence attached to these expectations. In practice, these two elements—the expected future spot price and the confidence attached to this expectation—cannot be separated. What exists is a probability distribution of expected future spot prices. This probability distribution generates the risk component of the premiums embedded in futures prices.

Option premiums—reflecting as they do the expected movement of prices (that is, the probability and magnitude of price changes)—are an indicator of uncertainty attached to expected future spot prices. Inasmuch as expectations about price movements (including the confidence attached thereto) convey information about the degree of uncertainty attached to expected future spot prices, option premiums are an indicator of the premiums embedded in futures.

Let us take an example. Suppose the January spot price of gold is 200, the September futures price is 230, and the call option premium on spot gold in September—with a striking price of 230—is 20. If the spot and futures prices were to remain constant, but the call option premium should increase to 25, this would suggest that a lower spot price is now expected (on average) in September, but at the same time greater uncertainty is now attached to this expectation (that is, a greater probability now exists that the future spot price will be above the striking price and/or the expected dispersion of possible future spot prices is now wider). The change in expectations (the mean expectation as well as confidence therein) is attributable to the constancy of the spot and futures price together with the increase in the option premium. Such change in expectations indicates that the premium embedded in the futures price has increased.

The distinction between mean expected future spot prices and the confidence with which such expectations are held is important, but has not received sufficient attention. Option markets provide useful information in this area. When account is taken of the variety of information about option contracts on a given asset (the different puts and calls) in conjunction with all the possible price changes in related markets, the value of information about options may be immense.

The economic value of information about option contracts is likely to be especially large for options on government debt securities, on bundles of private debt (or equity) securities, and on futures for such securities. Inflation tends to generate two related premiums on real interest rates: first, for the mean expected rate of inflation, and second, for the uncertainty attached to such expectations. By bringing information to bear on the degree of uncertainty surrounding expected inflation rates, option contracts also will tend to improve expectations about the most likely inflation rate. As a result, inflation premiums will tend to become both more objective and lower—thereby tending to reduce long-term interest rates. Such effects, over time, could be of some importance to the growth of our economy.

A reduction of interest rates not only has a direct impact on the cost of capital and level of wealth; it also has an indirect effect on the quantity and quality of market information. Reducing interest rates tends to generate lower premiums embedded in futures prices and lower premiums on options, as well as longer maturities of contracts for future transactions; these effects stem from the lower opportunity costs facing hedging firms and speculators. As a result, more and better market information about price expectations becomes available, and greater confidence attaches to this information. Such indirect effects of lower interest rates may be of some importance in an advanced stage of market development.

The substitution of objective—public or market—information for subjective, individual estimates on expected price movements (generated by option premiums) may well be of considerable value to firms with exposed positions in actuals or futures. Because options provide information about the uncertainty attached to future spot prices, they are likely to help objectify the risk of speculators in futures and thereby to reduce such risk. As a result, speculators' costs of carrying futures will be lower, and therefore the premiums embedded in futures prices will probably be lower.

This development means that the cost of hedging through futures is reduced. In addition, the cost of exposure to price uncertainty, and thereby the benefits of hedging through futures, is also likely to be reduced. Because the lower premiums embedded in futures are likely to be accompanied by greater confidence about their size, the market's expectation of future spot prices improves. In this way, the information generated by option premiums reduces price uncertainty and thereby the cost of exposure to price uncertainty.

Although the effect of options on the volume of hedging through futures is not clear, it is clear that commercial firms and speculators are able to assess better the benefits and costs of investments and that their costs of hedging and speculation are lower, with the result that their economic position is improved. Commercial firms and speculative investors may still make or lose money. However, in all likelihood, the magnitude of these gains or losses can be anticipated better. The closer coincidence of prior expectations and realized events means fewer surprises and unforeseen events. As a result, commercial firms and speculative investors will look more favorably upon the underlying spot assets and futures as mediums for investment. An expansion of such investments may allow the realization of economies of scale and attendant functional specialization.

One final comment here is in order. The improvement of market efficiency often is reflected in a reduction of "gaps" in prices or costs. For example, in the saving-investment process, the gap between the marginal efficiency of investment and the pure rate of interest tends to become smaller; in the case of securities, the premiums or discounts attaching to different maturities tend to become smaller; in spot markets as a whole, geographical differences and quality premiums (discounts) tend to diminish; in futures markets, backwardation (forwardation) tends to become smaller, and the like is true of implicit premiums in option markets. Although the gaps become smaller, they cannot be eliminated. Transaction costs and uncertainty—the foundation of such gaps—are inescapable; they can be reduced, but they cannot be eliminated. The gaps also tend to become more objective as markets become more efficient. Indeed, market development often entails a substitution of objective costs for subjective costs previously borne by one or both parties to a transaction.[19]

---

[19] Cf. J. R. Hicks, *Capital and Growth* (London: Oxford University Press, 1965), ch. 23; and Joseph M. Burns, "On the Effects of Financial Innovations," *Quarterly Review of Economics and Business*, vol. 11, no. 2 (summer 1971), pp. 83-95, esp. pp. 84-86.

6
Market Regulation

Not all markets are regulated by governmental agencies. And of those that are, regulations usually have come into existence after the emergence of the market.

Rationale of Market Regulation

Government regulation of markets is typically designed to assure the realization of the optimal benefits of markets (that is, the full potential benefits of markets taking into account the costs entailed in securing them). To achieve this objective, regulations have been designed to improve the orderly functioning, or operating efficiency, of markets.

Market regulation and market development do not occur in a vacuum. Thus, they should be studied and evaluated in the context of developments in the real sector of the economy, including nonregulatory governmental policies. The concluding chapter of this study discusses briefly some aspects of governmental policies as they affect the efficiency of markets and the tasks of regulatory agencies.

Regulation and Market Liquidity. Market regulations—whether for spot or future transactions—should be formulated within the context of a given market's liquidity. In particular, regulations should be designed to assure that orderliness of market conditions and quality of a market's organization—two aspects of a market's orderly functioning—are at the level warranted by the given market's liquidity. This does not mean that all disorderly conditions are to be precluded or that all imperfections in market organization are to be removed. Rather, it suggests, *inter alia*, that orderliness of market conditions and quality of market organization are of considerable importance in highly liquid markets, as is regulatory oversight of such markets.

Market conditions and organization are related in that high-quality organization fosters orderly conditions. They are also related in the sense that the ability to prevent disorderly markets is fostered by responsibility with regard to the quality of a market's organization. This relationship argues for market organization being a matter for regulatory concern if a regulatory agency exists.

In the more advanced free enterprise economies, with their intricate market interrelationships, the orderly functioning of markets is especially important. This importance extends to futures and option markets in addition to spot markets. The functioning of any one of these markets may be adversely or favorably affected by the orderliness of related markets. Indeed, just as the orderly functioning of a liquid market may have pervasive beneficial effects, so the malfunctioning of a liquid market may generate pervasive deleterious effects (as happened with the default on delivery of 50 million pounds of Maine potatoes on May 1976 futures contracts). In view of this, it would appear that greater regulatory attention should be focused on the more liquid markets than on the less liquid ones.

There has been some discussion to the effect that so-called thin markets are in need of special regulatory concern, and that measures to alleviate the thinness are warranted.[1] To be sure, illiquid markets pose a problem for both the users (direct and indirect) of these markets. Transaction costs tend to be high in all such markets. In addition, in illiquid markets for future transactions, forward or futures prices will often be poor estimators of future spot prices. These problems, however, do not necessarily justify special regulatory attention—unless an infant industry case can be made for subsidizing these markets' development or unless the markets lack liquidity because of artificial barriers. In fact, because illiquid markets are likely to have less influence on other markets, most of them deserve less regulatory attention than liquid markets. Some regulatory attention to illiquid markets is warranted, however, because they are probably more susceptible to manipulation (and thereby to disorderly conditions) than liquid ones.

Regulatory Costs. The history of market regulation has been somewhat controversial. In many instances, regulatory authorities appear

---

[1] See the proceedings of the North Central Regional Conference on Pricing Problems in the Food Industry (with Emphasis on Thin Markets), Commodity Futures Trading Commission, Washington, D.C., March 2, 1978.

to contribute to, rather than mitigate, disorderly market conditions. Indeed, it is important to recognize that regulation entails costs to the economy as well as benefits.

Regulatory costs may be of at least three types: administrative costs to the government and to market participants, inefficiencies in the rule-making process that may adversely affect the expectations of market participants, and needlessly burdensome or injurious regulations. Costs of the second and third types are part and parcel of the regulatory process, although they often become clear only with the passage of time. Even the most conscientious regulators may unwittingly confuse or mislead the market. In addition, when regulatory decisions have to be made, particularly when quick decisions appear to be necessary, the regulators cannot be sure of the effects of the rulings or of the burdens they may impose on the market.

Regulatory costs serve to constrain the role of market regulation. Unfortunately, regulatory agencies often tend to ignore such costs or to devote insufficient attention to them.

Emergence of Two Regulatory Agencies. In the United States, regulatory authority over spot markets is dispersed among many agencies. The securities markets are regulated by the Securities and Exchange Commission (SEC), as are option markets for corporate securities. The Commodity Futures Trading Commission (CFTC) regulates futures markets and options on commodities (spot and futures).

The SEC was established by the Securities Exchange Act of 1934 in response to widespread fraudulent activity in the securities industry. Over time, and especially in recent years, the SEC has devoted increasing attention to enhancing the quality of securities markets' organization.

The CFTC was established by the 1974 Amendments to the Commodity Exchange Act of 1936. The activities of the CFTC superseded those of the Department of Agriculture's Commodity Exchange Authority. Futures markets had gotten their start in the agricultural sector, but were spreading rapidly to other sectors of the economy. Not only had futures markets for assets other than agricultural commodities been established, but also new exchanges had been set up. The Department of Agriculture was simply not in a good position to regulate the burgeoning activity in futures. As with the SEC, the CFTC in its early years has been preoccupied with apparent fraudulent activities and price manipulation. As these problems are mitigated, the CFTC is likely to devote increasing attention to the quality of the markets' organization.

In general, as markets become increasingly liquid, the problem of disorderly conditions is likely to be reduced, inasmuch as liquidity militates against such conditions. As a result, the focus of regulatory attention is likely to shift from one of mitigating disorderly conditions to one of promoting the quality of market organization. Eventually, the quality of market organization may be such that less government regulation of markets will be needed. The design of the regulatory apparatus should be flexible enough to permit such a change.

In many respects, futures and options mark the most advanced stage of market development in a free enterprise economy. With effective regulation, these markets will help the free enterprise system realize its optimal potential for enhancing economic welfare.

Regulation of Futures

The principal function of the CFTC is to assure that the optimal benefits of futures markets are realized. To carry out this function, the commission seeks to mitigate, if not prevent, disorderly conditions in the markets and to improve the quality of the markets' organization. In the discussion, emphasis is placed on the benefits of regulation.

One prefatory comment on the commission's responsibility with regard to the adequacy of market liquidity is in order. The recent emergence of dual or multiple contracts on a given underlying asset, particularly financial instruments, is a problem of mounting concern. To be sure, contract competition can generate economic benefits, including the improvement of contract design. Such benefits, however, may not always be realizable; contract proliferation may impair the liquidity of existing markets and the adequacy of deliverable supplies of the underlying asset. If this happens, the optimal benefits of the markets will not be realized. This issue is likely to receive increasing regulatory attention.

Disorderly Market Conditions. Three types of disorderly market conditions are distinguishable: dissemination of deliberately false rumors, destabilizing trading activity, and monopoly situations.

Because futures markets are highly liquid, dissemination of deliberately false rumors is not much of a problem, except when such rumors derive from monopolies of information. Destabilizing trading activities also do not appear to pose a significant problem, because few artificial barriers to trading in futures exist.

Temporary monopolies. Futures markets are generally more competitive than most others; nevertheless, in certain situations, monopolies may bring about disorderly conditions in futures markets. For example, hedgers or speculators may hold monopolies of a temporary nature. These monopolies may result from a large degree of market power as well as from special market conditions such as warehouse fires, strikes in transportation industries, or other impediments to storage or delivery of supplies.

The exchanges and the CFTC have developed preventive and punitive approaches for dealing with temporary monopolies. The preventive approach is the preferred one. It seeks to remove the source of the problem or, if this is not possible, to take remedial measures to mitigate serious difficulties and prevent crises. The punitive approach is to enforce competitive conditions when and where competition breaks down.

The preventive removal of potential sources of problems includes appropriate specification of contract terms and conditions; this entails, *inter alia,* the number, location, and other characteristics of delivery points, the quality of grades that are deliverable, the price differentials for various grades, the quantity of the asset to be delivered, and the number and designation of contract months. Such specifications serve to facilitate commercial use of futures contracts and to foster a broad deliverable supply of commodities traded. Problem removal also includes periodic, and nearly continual, review of contract specifications to determine if commercial conditions in the spot market warrant new or revised specifications; release of public information bearing on the market (as soon as practicable, but after the close of business, to give the markets time to digest new information); and limitations on market positions.[2]

In addition to removing sources of potential problems, the preventive approach involves remedial actions to mitigate serious problems and prevent crises. In this connection, the exchanges or the commission may require an orderly liquidation of open positions if the exchange's or commission's market surveillance reveals that

---

[2] The commission's recent policy of restricting market power by limiting open positions of speculators in a given asset and the number of contracts in a given asset that a speculator can trade during a day appeared to be beset by several problems. First of all, it is difficult to make a practical distinction between speculators and hedgers, because virtually all of the commercial firms that engage in hedging operations also engage in speculation (in the broad sense of the term). Secondly, commercial firms as well as speculators may manipulate a market. Thirdly, the severity of the temporary monopoly problem is directly related to the proximity of potential deliveries. The commission is altering its policy in this area. In January 1979, daily trading limits for speculators were removed.

93

deliverable supplies may be inadequate to preserve competitive conditions. This action could avert a major crisis. Such action, however, should be taken with extreme care, inasmuch as it tends to affect the perceived and actual integrity of the market.

If a punitive approach is deemed necessary, the exchange and/or the commission may take legal action, such as securing injunctions or taking disciplinary steps, against entities to require that they conform with the rules of the exchange or the policies of the commission or the legislation of Congress.

Both approaches are carried out by the exchanges, subject to review by the commission. It is the commission's responsibility to see that the exchanges are carrying out their responsibilities in an efficient manner. The exchanges and the commission seek to maintain continual surveillance of the markets so as to be aware at the earliest possible time of any disorderly condition—actual or potential.[3]

Structural monopolies. The recent participation of foreign governments in futures markets could create a more serious monopoly problem than these temporary monopoly situations. Without appropriate regulation, such participation could distort the highly competitive nature of futures markets.

When foreign governments are allowed to trade in futures markets, the potential for market manipulation is great. Already, there is some indication that the coffee market may have been manipulated by El Salvador in 1977, and it is not impossible that other markets currently are being manipulated. Unless the commission takes effective action, market manipulation by foreign governments may occur in the future—and at an increasing rate. The economic history of this country is replete with examples of our government reacting to, rather than preventing, crises. It is important that the commission not become part of this history.

Foreign governments have diverse purposes for using futures markets. The reason Australia trades in wheat futures may differ from the reason Ghana trades in cocoa or Colombia in coffee. Some foreign governmental trading may be of a continuous nature, without benefit of inside information; other trading may be discrete and

---

[3] Central to the CFTC's surveillance efforts is information on the futures market positions of "large traders"—that is, traders that hold or control a position in a specific futures contract (or over a set of futures contracts for a given asset) that equals or exceeds a level specified by the commission. The idea is that large traders may have the potential to manipulate a market and therefore must be closely scrutinized. As a futures market becomes more liquid, the specified open interest (of a trader) that must be reported to the commission should increase. Such increases have in fact occurred.

occur only when a particular government entity has access to inside information.

Trading in futures by some foreign governments is ominous, because of their enormous power in the corresponding spot market. There are two aspects of this market power. First, some foreign governments have resources sufficient to carry out purchases or sales in a volume that could have a great effect on the price of an asset (typically a commodity). Such capability is inconsistent with a competitive environment, in which no single buyer or seller of a product could have a discernible influence on market price. This market power is not necessarily unique to foreign governments; it may also be possessed by some foreign private companies.

Second, and perhaps of greater significance, the foreign governments can impose quotas or tariffs on exports and imports, embargo shipments, impose taxes on or grant subsidies for the production or consumption of products, and join together in cartels to set prices. In addition, the governments may not communicate to the public their intentions to engage in any of these actions. In fact, a foreign government rationally might not wish to disseminate such information; public knowledge would likely militate against the effect that the government wishes to achieve.

The degree of market power that foreign governments have in spot markets for commodities differs greatly from one commodity to another. A government's power in a specific market is likely to be particularly great if the country controls a significant part of world production of that commodity. Even in the case of our domestic commodities, however, foreign governments could wield an extensive market influence from time to time.

In view of the power that some foreign governments have over spot prices of certain commodities (through their own policy actions or through the choice of information that they release, which information may or may not be accurate), their involvement in futures markets for these commodities could contribute further to their ability to extract large gains from their own market actions. Indeed, a foreign government may be able to build up positions surreptitiously in the futures market over a period of time without influencing materially the level of the futures price. When a foreign government eventually allows information on an asset (such as volume of output) to become public, the effect on the spot and futures prices can be pronounced, and the foreign government may reap huge earnings.

To the extent that a foreign government monopolizes market information about a commodity that it produces, its trading of the corresponding futures may generate disorderly conditions in the futures market. In addition, and perhaps of greater significance, once other participants in the market realize that a foreign government has a special informational advantage—which most people would view as inequitable—they will realize that their cost of hedging (or speculation) is now either higher or more uncertain, and consequently they will be more reluctant to use the market. The efficiency of the market is likely to suffer as a result.

The fact that foreign governments may be able, without interference by our government, to extract monopoly profits in U.S. spot markets should not—in and of itself—preclude remedying the situation in futures markets. Only if a foreign government's manipulative practices in futures markets mitigate the direct manipulation of spot prices might there be a case for a laissez-faire approach in futures markets. There is, however, no a priori reason for this situation to exist.

The existence of foreign private monopolies is also a problem for public policy in the United States. This problem should not, however, deter our efforts to alleviate the potentially more serious one of foreign governmental monopolies. It is unfortunate that many foreign countries do not have the stringent antitrust enforcement programs that exist in this country. In view of the recent rapid expansion of multinational companies, efforts to internationalize antitrust enforcement may well increase. The implementation, however, of such an international policy may be decades away.

Several alternative policies have been suggested to alleviate the problem posed by foreign governmental trading companies. Foreign governmental trading could be banned; such a policy does not appear desirable, however, in view of the benefits to futures markets from trading by many foreign governmental companies. Position limits and required notices to trade could be imposed on foreign governments; policies of this nature would probably do some good, but they only get at the symptoms of the problem, not its source.

An appropriate remedy for the foreign government trading problem would appear to be the publication, on a reasonably frequent basis, of data on positions of foreign governments in futures. Then, foreign governments would not be able to build up positions gradually and surreptitiously. The nongovernmental participants in the market would thus be in a better position to assess the risks in the market, and the level of futures prices would reflect this better assessment.

(At present, the commission receives less information on the position of foreign than of domestic traders.)

With frequent publication of open positions, some governments would not be able to extract as high earnings from their participation in the market as they currently do; futures prices would likely be bid up quicker in response to their purchases (and conversely for their sales). This quicker response—which would improve the allocation of resources—would probably reduce (but not eliminate) the participation of some foreign governments in the market, because their financial advantage would be reduced. However, not all foreign governments would be adversely affected by a publication requirement. The Australian Wheat Board and other foreign state companies of a similar nature probably would not be affected, inasmuch as few people have any basis for believing that such entities have monopoly power.

Controlling the undesirable element of foreign government participation in futures markets would enhance competition—actual and perceived—in these markets. The efficiency of the markets would be strengthened, and overall market participation would likely be higher in the long run.

In conclusion, it should be recognized that there may be at least two practical problems with publishing data on the positions of foreign governments in futures. First, it is not always easy to distinguish governmental and private foreign trading companies. Second, it may be difficult to publish the requisite data on a sufficiently frequent basis. These problems suggest that much work might have to be done if the commission were to approve in principle this approach.

Quality of Market Organization. The operating efficiency of futures markets depends not only on the orderliness of market conditions; it is affected also by the quality of institutional arrangements for servicing the markets—in particular, exchanges, futures commission merchants and clearinghouses.

Exchanges. Exchanges have a quasi-public status. They are given some privileges by virtue of the commission's approval of their contract designations; in turn, they are obligated to serve the public interest. The commission's responsibility is to assure that the exchanges are effectively serving the public interest. The commission carries out this responsibility by approving exchange rules as well as by requiring appropriate changes in existing rules and rule enforcement programs.[4] In addition, the commission may take disciplinary action against an exchange and/or its members.

Among the numerous issues involving the exchanges and their members, two appear to be especially important: dual trading (that is, the trading by exchange members for their own accounts as well as for their customers) and automation of trading. These issues are related in that automation of trading would likely affect the volume of dual trading.

Dual trading poses a problem because of the appearance, if not the occurrence, of a conflict of interest. The existence of such trading may weaken the integrity (actual or perceived) of markets. At least two approaches may be taken to this problem: dual trading could be banned, or exchanges could require (on their own or through CFTC regulations) that exchange members disclose to their customers information on their own trading activities. (Similar action toward nonmember futures commission merchants could be taken by the CFTC.)

Automation of trading poses a problem because the private interests of exchange members may differ from the public interest. This problem is not unique to futures exchanges; the same problem exists with regard to securities exchanges.

The benefits of automation are the subject of much dispute, because views differ about the effects of automation on market liquidity. To this writer, it would appear that automation would foster market liquidity by bringing improvements in information. Those who oppose automation often argue that floor traders, in the process of trading and conversing, add to market information and encourage trading.[5] To the extent that such trading fosters liquidity, it is of a short-run nature. Such benefits appear to be outweighed by the adverse long-run effects on the confidence of other participants—particularly the more knowledgeable ones—in the integrity of the market.

The introduction of automated trading would probably hurt floor traders. Floor traders, who may perform a brokerage function as well as trade for their own accounts, are now able to act on new market information more quickly than the public. New market information comes in two related forms: new data about market conditions (current or prospective) and current data on price, volume of trans-

---

[4] Under Sections 5a(12) and 8a(7), respectively, of the 1974 act.

[5] See Commodity Futures Trading Commission, *Automation in the Futures Industry*, proceedings of a conference sponsored by Commodity Futures Trading Commission, June 15, 1977, Washington, D.C.

actions, and—in the case of futures—open interest. Automated trading probably would reduce, if not eliminate, this advantage of floor traders.[6]

Any proposal to implement automation of trading must recognize that costs as well as benefits exist. The costs are likely to differ according to the way (including the time span) in which automation is implemented.

Futures commission merchants. The commission also has a responsibility to see that futures commission merchants are serving the public interest. An important issue involving the quality of futures commission merchants entails the integrity of customers' (direct users') funds. A crisis of confidence in the markets could occur if the integrity—actual or perceived—of customers' funds were impaired. A crisis of confidence would generate a disorderly market condition with adverse effects on market liquidity, in the long run as well as the short run.

In its market regulations, the commission thus has an important responsibility to protect the integrity of customers' funds. In its efforts to promote the quality of market conditions, the commission probably has enhanced the integrity of the marketplace and, thereby, the integrity of customers' funds. In addition, and more directly, the commission has issued regulations (such as those requiring registration of and minimum financial requirements for futures commission merchants, segregation of customers' funds from those of futures commission merchants, and disclosure of risk by futures commission merchants to their customers) that are designed to assure the integrity of customers' funds. In these ways, the commission has probably reduced the expected cost of default, thereby improving the efficiency of the market.

The exchanges' limitations on daily movements of futures prices, which are designed to ensure the financial integrity of member firms and clearinghouses, also may help protect the integrity of customers' funds. However, it is not clear that such limitations are serving a useful purpose on balance. Indeed, such limitations may be doing more harm than good. In particular, they may increase the cost of hedging at times when hedging is most needed (by locking commercial firms in or out of futures markets). In addition, they may impair the quality of information in futures markets.[7] If daily price limita-

---

[6] The "alarm" expressed by floor traders in futures markets at the prospect of automated trading supports this view.

[7] Ironically, daily price limitations are sometimes viewed as improving the quality of price information—by mitigating excessive optimism or excessive pessimism in

tions were lifted, margin requirements probably would be raised in order to protect clearinghouses and their customers. The effect of such changes in margin requirements should be considered in the context of the joint action.

Other Observations. As part of its responsibility to improve the working of futures markets, the commission gathers useful information and conducts research projects, which deal with futures markets and the commission's regulatory role. The 1974 act in fact requires the commission to "establish and maintain, as part of its ongoing operations, research and information programs. . . ." [Section 18] The commission has recently directed its attention to publishing data on futures.[8]

The commission's data indicate that the volume of transactions in futures and the level of open interest have increased dramatically in recent years. In addition, the futures market industry—that is, the institutions that service the markets—has also expanded rapidly. The commission's regulation of futures markets, including its actions to ensure the perceived and actual integrity of the markets, may have been partly responsible for these developments.

Regulation of Commodity Options

The 1974 CFTC Act, which amended the 1936 Commodity Exchange Act, continued the ban on trading options in those agricultural commodities whose futures were regulated by the late Commodity Exchange Authority. The 1974 act also provided for regulating futures of certain other assets and gave the CFTC the right to prohibit option trading in these assets or to allow it under rules and regulations that the commission might prescribe. The legislation gave the CFTC a similar choice with regard to any assets for which futures might subsequently come into existence.

Since its inception, the commission has been troubled by widespread fraudulent sales of option contracts on commodities—in particular, sales in this country of London options. This situation has adversely affected not only the perceived integrity of dealer options and London options but also that of related markets (particularly,

---

futures markets. This view does not appear warranted. It appears to reflect a preference for short-run price stability, but such preference only serves to heighten the instability of prices in the long run, as explained in Chapters 2 and 3.

[8] For example, see the data on futures markets in Commodity Futures Trading Commission, *Annual Report 1977*.

spot and futures markets in the underlying assets). For these reasons, as well as the commission's limited resources, the commission in June 1978 suspended—with a few exceptions—the sale of commodity options in this country. The purchase or sale of options by commercial firms—so-called trade options—were not suspended; and some dealer options were permitted. In the Futures Trading Act of 1978, Congress imposed a ban—also with a few exceptions—on all commodity option transactions until the CFTC presents evidence of its ability to regulate such transactions.

The commission is in the process of drawing up regulations for the inception of option trading in .those commodities whose futures came under regulation in 1974 or thereafter. Upon completion of a three-year pilot program, the commission is expected to consider an ongoing program of option trading on U.S. exchanges. The inception of the pilot program may be accompanied by a relaxation of the restrictions on off-exchange commodity options in this country. Just as futures improve the working of forward markets, so exchange-traded options likely will improve the functioning of off-exchange markets. Such improvement should help the commission deal with abuses in the sale of off-exchange options. To be sure, the full benefits of the competition will not be realized immediately; it may take some time for the public to understand fully the advantages of options traded on U.S. exchanges. Although dealer options are likely to decline in importance in the face of the new, competitive challenge, they will probably still serve a useful economic purpose—both as an innovative device and as an instrument for trading those assets for which an organized market may not be economically feasible.

Historically, there has been a lot of controversy involving futures and options, much of it centering on the role of speculators—a role that is little understood or is misunderstood.[9] Because speculators may well hold a larger percentage of open interest in options than in futures, it is important to clarify the economic usefulness of options and speculators' contributions to this usefulness.

A pilot program should be helpful in clarifying the magnitude and type of economic benefits of options, as well as the benefits and costs of the commission's rules and regulations governing options. In devising a pilot program, the commission is expected to give

---

[9] Goss and Yamey state, "Futures trading has often been controversial. . . . Public concern has focused on the supposed effects of futures trading (and of the speculation which it facilitates) on the level and movement of the prices of the traded commodities." "Introduction: The Economics of Futures Trading" in *The Economics of Futures Trading*, ed. B. A. Goss and B. S. Yamey (New York: Halstead Press, 1976), p. 1.

attention to the types of data that will be needed to assess the economic benefits of options and the usefulness of the commission's option trading rules and regulations. In the pilot program, the commission probably will allow option trading only on those assets that have a large deliverable supply, accurate data on such supplies, and a reliable mechanism for determining their price. For options on futures, the commission probably will require that the expiration date be about two weeks before the maturity date of the underlying futures. This would reduce the probability of price manipulation; it would also, however, reduce the benefits of some users of such options.

Some of the problems of futures trading, such as the foreign trader issue and market concentration in maturing contracts, are also likely to exist in the case of options. In fact, these problems in futures—if left alone—may well be exacerbated by trading in options. It would be advantageous if these issues were resolved prior to the adoption of the pilot program of option trading on exchanges.

The importance of anticipating problems in option markets is underscored by Alfred Marshall's insightful concern about option trading. Marshall stated, "There are a few cases in which dealings in options are part of legitimate trade. But there appears to be more force in the arguments for prohibiting them by law, than for prohibiting a simple buying or selling of futures; for they are relatively more serviceable to the gambler and the manipulator than to the straightforward dealer." [10] To be sure, the benefits to commercial firms of options are far greater today than at the time that Marshall was writing, inasmuch as the volume of risk exposure in actuals and futures has grown dramatically during the twentieth century; and the possibility of price manipulation is much less today than in Marshall's time, inasmuch as the underlying spot and futures markets are much more liquid. Nevertheless, Marshall's concern about the comparative advantage of price manipulation in options is correct. Indeed, options are more serviceable to the manipulator than are futures because of the greater return on capital (owing to the greater leverage), for a given degree of manipulation of the underlying asset's price.

Boundaries of CFTC Jurisdiction

In the 1974 act that created the CFTC, Congress gave the commission exclusive jurisdiction over futures markets. Congress also gave the commission jurisdiction over other kinds of "commodity" transactions

---

[10] Alfred Marshall, *Industry and Trade* (London: MacMillan and Co., 1927), p. 257, note 1.

(option transactions and "leveraged" sales of gold and silver), and some responsibility in spot markets of assets traded on futures markets. This section discusses the commission's jurisdiction over futures markets and its responsibility in spot markets.

Futures Markets. The 1974 CFTC Act states:

> . . . that the [Commodity Futures Trading] Commission shall have exclusive jurisdiction with respect to accounts, agreements (including any transaction which is of the character of, or is commonly known to the trade as, an "option" . . .), and transactions involving contracts of sale of a commodity for future delivery, traded or executed on a contract market . . . or any other board of trade, exchange, or market. . . . [Section 2(a)(1)]

The intent of this provision was to vest exclusive jurisdiction over commodity futures trading in a single agency, the Commodity Futures Trading Commission.

In addition, the act states that the word "commodity" shall include not only agricultural products but also "all other goods and services, except onions . . ., and all other services, rights, and interests in which contracts for future delivery are presently or in the future dealt in. . . ." [Section 2(a)(1)]. The intent of this provision was to cover all futures trading that then existed or might develop in the future, except for onions. The exception can hardly be justified and warrants removal.

The principal reason that Congress granted the CFTC exclusive jurisdiction over all futures trading was to avoid contradictions or duplications between regulations of the CFTC and those of the SEC or of state regulatory agencies.[11] Regulation of a single form of trading by two or more agencies, besides being wasteful, can generate confusion and uncertainty. For a market in which expectations and confidence are important, uncertainty from diffused jurisdiction is especially troublesome; it has adverse effects on the cost of speculation and hedging, and thereby on the efficiency of markets.

Congress may also have granted the CFTC exclusive jurisdiction because the SEC had apparently discouraged the development of a futures market that was potentially in the public interest. In 1972, the Federal Home Loan Bank Board sought SEC approval of a futures market for Government National Mortgage Association (GNMA)

---

[11] Some of the material in the remainder of this subsection is based on an unsigned article to which this writer contributed, "Issues in the CFTC's Sunset Review," *Journal of Regulation* (May 1978).

securities. The SEC did not respond favorably. Subsequently, after the CFTC was created, the Chicago Board of Trade requested contract designation in GNMAs. The CFTC approved this contract, and trading began in October 1975. This new market instrument seems to be serving a useful economic purpose. The SEC apparently was also reluctant to approve the concept of a futures contract based on a stock price index, such as the Dow Jones Industrial Average. A futures contract on a broad-based equity security has since been proposed to the CFTC. (An evaluation of this proposal is contained in Appendix C.)

Congress may well have recognized that its grant of authority to the CFTC logically extended to all option trading, including that of equity securities. However, options on equity securities were already under SEC regulation, and Congress precluded the CFTC from entering an area that was already under SEC regulation.[12]

Recently, the CFTC's exclusive jurisdiction in futures markets has been the subject of much debate. The focus of this debate was the 1978 Congressional "sunset" review of, and reauthorization hearings on, the CFTC—the first such review and reauthorization of a regulatory agency. During this review, the SEC, the Treasury, and the Office of Management and Budget, among others, raised questions about the CFTC's jurisdiction over futures. The CFTC's exclusive jurisdiction was in fact one of the most important, if not the most important, issue in the review.

On February 7, 1978, the SEC in a letter to the General Accounting Office recommended that the regulation of financial futures be transferred to the SEC. In addition, the SEC indicated a willingness to absorb all CFTC responsibilities if Congress so wished. The possibility of contradictory or duplicative regulations renders the SEC's transfer recommendation undesirable.

A merger of the SEC and the CFTC is a different issue and warrants serious attention. This consolidation might promote regulatory efficiency in a number of ways; for example, brokerage houses would be regulated by only one government agency, costs of regulating options would be reduced, and the regulation of the burgeoning financial instrument futures might be improved. The crucial issue, however, is whether a consolidated agency would provide the appropriate framework for recognizing the benefits and costs of trading

---

[12] Cf. John V. Rainbolt II, "Regulating the Grain Gambler and His Successors," Symposium on Commodity Futures Regulation, *Hofstra Law Review*, vol. 6, no. 1 (Fall 1977), pp. 24-25.

in futures. At this time, such a framework does not appear to be appropriate.

Shortly after the SEC letter, the Treasury Department requested joint jurisdiction with the CFTC in regulating futures markets for U.S. government securities. The Treasury advanced two principal reasons for its proposal: to assure the efficient financing of these securities, and to assure the efficient functioning of spot markets for them.

The Treasury's arguments are questionable. The first reason for its proposal—a desire to assure "efficient" (to the Treasury, this usually means low-cost) financing of U.S. government securities—is understandable. However, this desire argues against a Treasury role in regulating the futures markets of government securities. There would be an apparent, if not actual, conflict of interest if the Treasury had the responsibility of issuing securities and at the same time had the responsibility of regulating a futures market for such securities. For example, the Treasury, finding that interest rates embedded in Treasury futures were moving up, and fearing an effect of such movement on spot interest rates, might in some way limit or even suspend trading in these futures.

This problem is reminiscent of Treasury's pre-1951 dispute with the Federal Reserve. Treasury was successful in exerting pressure on the Federal Reserve to maintain stable prices in spot markets of government securities in order to assure what it viewed as the "efficient" financing of such securities. As a result of this policy, the entire Treasury debt was in effect monetized, and inflation followed.

Alarmed by the flow of events, Senator Paul Douglas brought about the Accord of 1951, which reaffirmed the Federal Reserve's independence and its responsibility in spot markets of government securities. Since then, for practical purposes, the Federal Reserve's only obligation to Treasury has been not to thwart or hinder Treasury debt management operations; the Federal Reserve is not obligated to take any positive action to facilitate Treasury operations. It is interesting to note that the Federal Reserve's mandate to its staff switched in 1951 from a policy of "maintaining orderly markets" (which had been interpreted by the Treasury as one of maintaining low interest rates) to one of "preventing disorderly markets."[13]

---

[13] In the 1974 CFTC Act, the commission was given the same mandate in the futures markets area that the Federal Reserve had given to its staff in the spot market area—namely, the prevention of disorderly markets. The commission's neutral position with regard to the level of futures prices may be more strongly entrenched than the Federal Reserve's position with regard to spot prices in

Treasury's second reason for its proposal—a desire to assure the efficient functioning of spot markets in U.S. government securities—is also understandable. The efficient functioning of such markets facilitates the issuance of new Treasury debt. The fact of the matter is that Treasury has no direct regulatory responsibility in such spot markets; for practical purposes, Treasury's only role is advisory. Thus, it may in effect be seeking jurisdiction in the regulation of futures markets on the basis of an erroneous assumption—namely, that it has jurisdiction in the regulation of the spot market.

The relationship between futures markets and the efficiency of corresponding spot markets—whether in government securities or any other asset—is a matter of considerable importance to the CFTC. Both economic theory and empirical evidence indicate that futures markets enhance the efficiency of corresponding spot markets, as happened in the case of GNMAs. Spot markets in other government securities should also become (or in a few cases, may already have become) more liquid with the introduction and development of futures markets.

To be sure, if a futures market were to be introduced for a U.S. government security in which deliverable supply was of questionable adequacy—either because the security was subject to call or to early redemption or for some other reason—the spot market might well be subjected to disorderly conditions. This possibility suggests that proposed futures contracts for such securities must be analyzed carefully to ascertain their viability in commercial usage. Needless to say, the U.S. Treasury can, and should, play an important advisory role in such analysis.

Other agencies that regulate or have expertise in the market of the actual asset or produce the actual asset may also be concerned about the impact of futures and option trading on the underlying asset. These concerns also can and should be dealt with through consultation among the interested agencies. A legislative requirement for such consultation—particularly with the SEC, Federal Reserve, Treasury, and Department of Agriculture—could be helpful, provided it did not lead to unwarranted delays in the regulatory process. Such a requirement was in fact promulgated in the Futures Trading Act of 1978.

---

view of the latter institution's additional responsibilities in the spot market area (namely, the conduct of monetary policy). Indeed, almost inevitably, political pressures are brought to bear—directly or indirectly—on the conduct of monetary policy. It is a tribute to the Federal Reserve that the importance of its independence (in fact as well as in name) appears to be increasingly realized.

Closely related to the issue of exclusive jurisdiction is whether regulatory power should be lodged in an independent agency or the executive branch. The Office of Management and Budget, at a very late stage in the congressional review, suggested that the CFTC's status as an independent agency be ended and that its functions be transferred to a new unit in the executive branch. One segment of the futures industry has advocated the return of futures regulation to the Department of Agriculture. This proposal poses a fundamental problem: whether the objectives of futures market regulation are compatible with the department's role in influencing the level of agricultural prices. The proposal also ignores the developments that were in part responsible for the creation of the commission—the burgeoning of the use of futures well beyond agricultural commodities.

Most participants of the futures industry favor continuing the independent and exclusive status of the CFTC, at least until more experience can be gained; the Futures Trading Act of 1978, in fact, continued this status.

Spot Markets. The 1974 CFTC Act defines the commission's responsibility in spot markets as follows: "The Commission may conduct regular investigations of the market of goods, articles, services, rights, and interests which are the subject of futures contract. . . ." [Section 16(a)]. This provision gives the CFTC some responsibility in spot markets of assets that are the subject of futures contracts. This arrangement appears to be sound in view of the inherent interrelationship of spot and futures markets.

The commission has the responsibility to see that futures prices are not distorted. Without high quality spot price information, the commission, as well as the exchanges, are at a disadvantage in identifying price distortions in futures markets. For this reason, the quality of spot price information is an integral part of the commission's surveillance program. Because the development of futures markets improves the quality of spot prices, the commission's surveillance responsibility in spot markets is likely to be facilitated over time by the expansion of futures markets.

The commission has a special responsibility with regard to spot price quotation committees on futures exchanges. The activities of these committees are subject to review by the commission as part of its general authority to regulate exchanges. In particular, the commission must approve the rules and procedures under which these committees operate. In this approval process, the commission is directed to "take into consideration the public interest to be protected by the antitrust laws and endeavor to take the least anti-competitive means" of achieving the objectives, policies, and purposes of the 1974 act (Section 15). This directive applies not only to the approval of contract rules submitted by exchanges, but also to any exchange rules that the commission may require [Sections 5(a)(12) and 8(a)(7)].

In early 1977, the commission reviewed the rules and practices of all spot price quotation committees then in existence on exchanges. Such committees existed on the Minneapolis Grain Exchange, the Kansas City Board of Trade, and the New York Coffee and Sugar Exchange.

The commission used two approaches in its review. First, it examined the operating procedures of the committees to see whether they are conducive to good quality data. Attention was paid to whether the procedures were such that the commission, in approving them, was meeting its responsibility under the act—particularly, whether the procedures were the "least anticompetitive means" of achieving the purposes of the act. In this connection, an important issue was whether the committees were exercising more discretion (in arriving at price quotations) than was necessary to maintain a useful price information system. Second, the commission examined the quality of the spot committees' data and studied the extent to which the data are used. The two approaches are related in that efficient and equitable committee operating procedures foster high quality, usable data.

The commission's staff report indicated that no hard and fast standards can be applied either to the nature of spot price quotation data or to appropriate spot price committee operations.[14] Commodities differ greatly in nature, and operating procedures that may seem appropriate in one situation may not seem appropriate in another. As a case in point, of the three exchanges whose committee operations were the subject of the inquiry, the two grain exchanges provide an organized market for spot trading in certain commodities, whereas the New York Coffee and Sugar Exchange does not. This difference in exchange practices reflects, at least in part, a difference in the nature of commodity transactions; many of the grains are traded on a reasonably continuous basis, whereas sugar transactions typically occur at

[14] Commodity Futures Trading Commission, Office of Chief Economist, *Inquiry into Operations of Spot Price Committees on New York Coffee and Sugar Exchange, Minneapolis Grain Exchange, and Kansas City Board of Trade* (Washington, D.C.: Commodity Futures Trading Commission, June 1977).

discrete intervals. These differences were important factors considered by the commission in its evaluation of the committees.

The commission's staff report indicated that the committees' spot price information was, in general, useful to the conduct of commercial business; this suggests that retaining the committees is desirable. The study indicated, however, that some of the committees on all three exchanges were exercising more discretion than is necessary to provide useful price information systems. An area of concern to the commission included procedures for quoting prices when no transactions occurred. The absence of effective written guidelines for the committees' operations contributed to the commission's concerns. As a result, it appeared that the commission could not carry out its responsibility under the 1974 act if it approved some of the rules and practices of the committees.

The commission's staff made a series of recommendations to the commission. The recommendations were an attempt to get at committee problems the staff perceived. The commission approved the staff's recommendations in June 1977. Subsequently, the commission's staff proceeded to work with the exchanges to improve committee procedures and guidelines.

In the meantime, the U.S. Department of Justice brought suit against the New York Coffee and Sugar Exchange—alleging that the way in which spot sugar prices had been quoted by its spot price quotation committees had violated antitrust laws since 1970. At that point, many of the spot committees on the three exchanges disbanded. In December 1978, the Justice Department filed a proposed consent decree that would settle the suit. The exchange has approved the proposed settlement, which would provide for sugar industry representatives to be contacted at random from a roster of names for their views on the basis (the difference between spot and futures prices). The proposed settlement is subject to approval by a federal district court in New York. A settlement (consistent with commission policies) would be useful inasmuch as information on spot sugar prices is of value to the sugar industry.

7

Concluding Observations

This study has explored some fundamental principles about the development and ramifications of spot, futures, and option markets. It has also examined the rationale for regulating these markets. It is useful to recognize that both the development of markets and their regulation take place within a given institutional environment, including governmental policies.

This final chapter addresses itself briefly to two issues: the effects of governmental policies on market efficiency, and the continuing barrage of public criticism of futures and option markets in the face of their widespread public benefits.

Effects of Governmental Policies on Market Efficiency

Governmental policies inevitably affect market efficiency. Policies in such areas as antitrust enforcement as well as market news reports and data typically tend to enhance market efficiency. Policies involving the protection of property rights are also capable of enhancing market efficiency, but policies in this area have been sadly deficient in recent years. And policies that directly affect demand-supply conditions in a market often impair market efficiency.

Two aspects of governmental policy may be distinguished: the substance of the policy, and the nature of deliberations thereon. With regard to the latter, governmental policy that is clear and predictable is conducive to orderly market conditions; policy that is ambiguous (whether because of indecision, vacillation, or obfuscation) usually impairs market conditions, and thereby market efficiency. Futhermore, the increasingly large role of government in the economy—relative to GNP as well as absolutely—means that ambiguity in governmental policy has larger adverse effects today than in previous decades.

Historically, governments have often sought to stabilize prices in some spot markets, either through explicit price stabilization schemes or through the prevention of alleged disorderly conditions. Such efforts usually preclude the adjustment of resources to changes in underlying market conditions. In general, impediments to price changes (partial or total), and thus to resource adjustments, eventually necessitate larger price changes and resource adjustments than would otherwise have occurred. As a result, price instability and uncertainty increase over the long run.

Governmental efforts to stabilize spot prices impair the efficiency of futures markets; the increase of short-run price stability reduces commercial demand for near-term hedging, and the increase of long-run price instability and uncertainty reduces speculators' willingness to assume open positions in distant-term futures contracts. In addition, in view of uncertainty about the timing and the magnitude of the eventual price changes, disorderly conditions may arise in spot markets. It is indeed somewhat paradoxical that the government, which wishes in many cases to improve the flow of information to the private sector, frequently adds to uncertainty in the private sector by being silent about its own actions—for example, whether or not it is intervening in markets and, if so, when and on what scale.

Governmental efforts to stabilize spot prices represent a bias in favor of short-run or commercial considerations. Such efforts, however, lead to a bias against long-run or risk investment considerations. Over the long run, with an increase of price uncertainty and a diminution of capital investment, even commercial interests may be hurt by such governmental actions. Commercial interests are directly hurt when governmental attempts to maintain price stability or to limit price variability break down, as they generally do. Indeed, even the rather innocuous International Tin Agreement, long considered the exception to the rule, broke down in early 1977. Appendix A discusses the comparative advantages of fixed and floating exchange rates for trade and capital investment.

In addition to trying to stabilize some spot prices, governments have often sought to curb rates of increase of domestic price levels, either directly (by fiat) or indirectly (by moral suasion). Such efforts also tend to preclude the adjustment of resources to changes in underlying market conditions. In general, they also eventually necessitate larger price changes and resource adjustments than would otherwise have occurred. The resulting increase of price instability and uncertainty tend to impair the efficiency of spot and futures markets.[1]

---

[1] In evaluations of price controls, the impairment of efficiency of futures markets

Ironically, the adverse effects of governmental excesses in fiscal and/or monetary policy tend to be masked temporarily by price controls, and the consequences of continuing such excesses are not as apparent as they otherwise would be. Governmental excesses in fiscal and/or monetary policy tend to generate inflationary conditions that lead to greater price instability and uncertainty.[2] These effects of inflation impair the efficiency of markets for spot transactions, but they particularly affect those for future transactions.

These long-run costs of inflationary governmental policies, together with the slow but steady erosion of property rights, have not received sufficient attention by policy makers. This is partly because the political process has a short-run orientation.[3] It also reflects a lack of understanding of the role of free markets and of speculators' contributions to that role.[4] It is useful to recognize the benefits of

usually is neglected. In addition to the adverse effects on the efficiency of futures markets, controls may alter the maturity structure of futures prices. Through the creation of asymmetric expectations about the level of future prices, controls induce speculators to take straddle positions—selling near-term futures and buying more distant-term ones. Such speculation tends to reduce spot prices, thereby worsening the shortage of supplies that usually exists during price controls.

Controls usually are not placed on prices of assets traded on futures markets. In 1973, however, controls were placed on the prices of livestock products, and livestock is traded on futures markets. During the 1973 period, it appeared to take about two weeks for the maturity structure of these futures prices to reflect fully the effects of the price controls. Later, the announcement of decontrols also appeared to generate price effects in these futures markets over a two-week period.

If price controls are placed on such assets again (or on other assets for which futures markets exist), the effects on the maturity structure of future prices may well occur more quickly, inasmuch as the 1973 experience will improve speculators' understanding. If, however, for assets on which futures exist, the market expects price controls with greater confidence today than in early 1973, then more of the effects of price controls on futures markets (both on market efficiency and on the maturity structure of prices) are already with us, and fewer effects will occur with a formal announcement. This, unfortunately, is one of the legacies of the 1973 experience.

[2] Several studies have shown a positive correlation between the magnitude of inflation and the degree of price instability (micro and macro). See, for example, Richard W. Parks, "Inflation and Relative Price Variability," *Journal of Political Economy*, vol. 86, no. 1 (January/February 1978), pp. 79-95; and Benjamin Klein, "Our New Monetary Standard: The Measurement and Effects of Price Uncertainty, 1880-1973," *Economic Inquiry*, vol. 13, no. 4 (December 1975). The increase of commodity option premiums since the mid-1960s, noted earlier, lends support to the findings of these studies.

[3] The short-run bias inherent in the structure of the political process is not likely to change in the near future. However, it would not be surprising to see eventually an increase in the terms of office for members of the U.S. House of Representatives (to perhaps four years) and for the president (to perhaps six years), and at the same time a limitation on the president to one term and to members of the House and Senate to perhaps twelve years.

[4] The lack of understanding of the speculator's role is sharply revealed when government takes actions to "hurt" and "punish" speculators.

the flexibility and resiliency of free markets, especially financial ones. This flexibility fosters the flow of information to commercial firms and helps them adjust to changes in their environment.

It is, indeed, unfortunate that at a time in history when technology is such that free markets could be adding immeasurably to the economic vitality of our nation, our government has been impeding the working of our markets. It is a tribute to our markets—to their ingenuity, resiliency, and strength—that they have been able to survive and even to grow and develop in the face of governmental impediments.

The impact of events (especially high and uncertain rates of inflation) and of certain economic writings (especially those of Milton Friedman) during the past generation are helping to correct the prevailing bias in governmental policy.[5] We have recently witnessed some movement towards freer market determination of interest rates and of foreign exchange rates. In the case of debt securities, the greater role of the free market is attributable to the Federal Reserve's increased emphasis—since 1970—on the behavior of the money supply and its somewhat smaller concern with the behavior of interest rates.[6] In the foreign exchange area, the greater role of the free market stems from the abandonment—in 1973—of an adjustable peg system of fixed rates. It is no accident that futures contracts have recently emerged in both of these markets. Such contracts were prompted by increased demand—commercial and speculative—associated with freer markets.[7]

---

[5] For example, see Milton Friedman, *Essays in Positive Economics* (University of Chicago Press: Chicago, 1953); idem, *A Program for Monetary Stability* (Fordham University Press: New York, 1957); idem, *Capitalism and Freedom* (University of Chicago Press: Chicago, 1962); and idem, with Anna Schwartz, *A Monetary History of the United States* (Princeton University Press: Princeton, 1963).

[6] In connection with Milton Friedman's views on monetary policy, it may be useful to note that his advocacy of monetary rules has an advantage—not widely recognized—over and above the direct effects arising out of the long and variable lags: rules tend to reduce uncertainty, and investors will not have to be faced with guessing when money supply changes will moderate the cycle and when they will accentuate the cycle. Thus, even if discretionary money supply changes serve to moderate the cycle approximately 50 percent of the time, and even if the degree of expected moderation is the same (on balance) as the degree of expected accentuation, such changes may thus still have adverse effects. With regard to monetary rules, it is, however, important that they not be inflexible, so that they are able to take into account special situations in the short run and structural changes in the long run.

[7] Both of these futures markets had their antecedents in forward markets. For debt securities, the forward market is implicit in the term structure of interest rates; for foreign currencies, the forward market consists of an interbank market.

Public Criticism of Futures and Option Markets

In view of the public benefits of futures and option markets, it is somewhat paradoxical that they are the targets of an almost continuing barrage of public criticism. And although the benefits of these markets are similar to those of spot markets, it is also somewhat strange that the focus of public criticism has been largely on futures and option markets.

These public attitudes challenge explanation. Organized spot markets developed rapidly during the closing decades of the eighteenth and during the nineteenth centuries. This development occurred at a time when markets were quite free and competitive, and when economic theorists—beginning with Adam Smith—were busy extolling the virtues of free markets. In contrast, futures and option markets developed rapidly during the closing decades of the nineteenth and during the twentieth centuries. Their development occurred at a time when markets had become less free and less competitive and when economic theorists were frequently inclined to question the benefits of free markets. This period also witnessed the Great Depression, the publication of Keynes's *General Theory*, a more critical attitude towards business and profits, and a more activist governmental approach to economic and social problems (perceived as well as actual).

In short, the rapid development of futures and option markets occurred in a greatly different environment from that in which rapid development of organized spot markets occurred. This difference may partly account for the more intense public suspicion and criticism of futures and option markets than of spot markets.

In addition, futures and option markets tend to enhance the variability of spot prices in the short run; and thus speculators, who contribute greatly to the viability of these markets, serve to accentuate the short-run swings in spot prices. With policy officials so concerned about short-run phenomena, it is not surprising that futures markets and speculators are so often vilified.

Futures and option markets also improve information about the effects of governmental policy on demand-supply conditions. To the extent that information is so improved, it becomes more difficult for government to obtain short-run benefits from macroeconomic policies at the risk of long-run damage to the economy. For example, if the federal budget deficit or money supply is increased sharply with a view to accelerating an ongoing economic expansion in the short run, the futures contracts for debt securities are likely to register rather promptly an increase in interest rates. Such increases tend to spill over quickly to the spot markets for securities. The real economy will therefore expand less than it otherwise would have, while the general price level will tend to respond more promptly. This development places another burden on the short-run orientation of policy officials. Recognition of this burden may well prompt attacks by such officials on futures and option markets.[8]

Similarly, futures markets for foreign exchange may hasten the decline of spot exchange rates in the face of some sharp stimulation through fiscal or monetary actions. The quicker decline in the international value of the dollar may place still another burden on the short-run orientation of policy officials, and may also prompt attacks by such officials on futures markets (as well as on floating exchange rates).

Furthermore, unlike the organization of spot markets, the formal organization of futures markets requires regulatory approval. Those who oppose organization of a new market can express their disapproval in a recognized public forum. Because futures markets always present something of a threat to entrenched interests, producers and large dealers whose market positions may be threatened usually oppose new futures markets. We have recently witnessed such opposition in the case of zinc, rice, aluminum, nickel, coal, and the financial and foreign currency futures. The opposition usually is well organized, and the attacks frequently center on speculators—always a popular target.

The irony is that futures markets are a catalyst in intensifying competition in spot markets. According to Alfred Marshall's theory of countervailing power (popularized by John Kenneth Galbraith), bigness on one side of a market breeds bigness on the other.[9] There is, however, another theory of countervailing power—namely, that the market power of large firms is in time reduced, and that this development occurs through gains in market efficiency at least partly occasioned by futures markets.

---

[8] At the same time, however, such recognition eventually may prompt policy officials to seek long-run policy measures, such as overhaul of an antiquated tax system that impairs saving and investment, to cope with structural problems in the economy. In fact, futures and option markets will expedite the realization of the beneficial effects from such policies.

[9] Alfred Marshall stated: "monopolistic combinations in one branch of industry foster the growth of monopolistic combinations in those which have occasion to buy from or sell to it: and the conflicts and alliances between such associations play a role of ever increasing importance in modern economics." Alfred Marshall, *Principles of Economics*, Ninth Edition (New York: Macmillan Co., 1961), vol. 1, bk. 5, ch. 14, sec. 9, p. 493.

It appears unlikely that the public will soon have a right understanding of the benefits of futures and option markets and of speculators' contributions thereto. Over time, however, such an understanding is probably inevitable. Once the public does become aware of the benefits of futures and option markets and of the role of speculation, a new economic order may come into being—one that will be conducive not only to the expansion of trade but also to that of capital investment. Such an economic order would spell gains in the vitality and dynamism of our system of free enterprise.

APPENDIX A

Fixed and Floating Exchange Rate Systems: Their Comparative Advantages for Trade and Investment

A lot of controversy surrounds the current system of floating exchange rates. Perhaps the most important aspect of the controversy is the system's effect on international trade and investment compared with that of fixed exchange rates.

This note shows that floating exchange rates have a comparative advantage in promoting international investment and that fixed exchange rates (adjustable peg) have a comparative advantage in promoting international trade. This result emerges from an analysis of foreign exchange risks—distant-term and near-term—and the cost of hedging these risks under both types of exchange rate system.

The note also discusses a crucial issue involving the comparative advantage of floating rates—namely, the nature of governmental policy response to exchange rate problems. Because of initial policy reactions to exchange rate movements under a floating rate system, the initial benefits of floating rates (and hence the system's comparative advantage) are not likely to be as pronounced as they will ultimately become.[1]

Foreign Exchange Risk

The switch to floating rates is likely to affect the cost to firms of being exposed to exchange rate risk. For distant-term exposure, the cost to firms is likely to be reduced; for near-term exposure, the effect on firms' cost is less clear.

Under floating rates, uncertainty about distant-term exchange rates is likely to be lowered because of the expected smaller variation

---

[1] This appendix is based on material in chapter 3 of the author's study, *Accounting Standards and International Finance: with Special Reference to Multinationals* (Washington, D.C.: American Enterprise Institute, 1976).

119

in rates for given underlying economic conditions (including government policies). Indeed, as Milton Friedman pointed out, real adjustments are being made continually in response to changes in exchange rates, rather than being postponed, as they usually are under fixed rates. This postponement eventually necessitates larger changes in exchange rates, which compel larger real adjustments.[2]

How the switch to floating rates affects uncertainty about near-term exchange rates is not clear; it depends on the type of prior experience under fixed rates (little uncertainty or crisis). If we could compare the entire experience under the Bretton Woods regime with what the experience would have been under floating rates during the Bretton Woods years, we would probably find that uncertainty about near-term exchange rates would have been higher under floating rates than that which actually existed (on balance) under fixed rates.

To complete the analysis of near-term uncertainty, however, we would have to compare the recent experience under floating rates with what experience under fixed rates (adjustable peg) would have been. This recent period has witnessed great financial problems generated by large and divergent changes in government macroeconomic policies and by the oil crisis. It is likely that near-term uncertainty during this period would have been greater under fixed rates than it has been under floating rates. Indeed, the breakdown of the fixed-rate system was occasioned by the system's inability to deal with recent international financial problems.

The Cost of Hedging

Firms may reduce their exposure to foreign exchange risk by hedging their positions in actuals through offsetting positions in forward or futures contracts. We would expect the cost of hedging distant-term exposure to be lower under floating rates than under fixed rates, and the cost of hedging near-term exposure to be generally higher.

The cost of hedging consists of transaction costs and costs of carrying a position in the forward (or futures) market. The latter consists primarily of default risk and premiums embedded in forward or futures rates (the difference between the expected future spot rate and the current forward or futures rate).[3] The switch to floating rates would reduce the cost of distant-term hedging if speculators become more certain about distant-term future spot rates. Speculators are

---

[2] See Milton Friedman, "The Case for Flexible Exchange Rates," in idem, *Essays in Positive Economics* (Chicago: University of Chicago Press, 1953).

[3] See Chapter 3 of this study.

TABLE A-1

Price Quotations and Spreads in Interbank Foreign Exchange Market

(in dollars per unit of foreign currency)

Currency and Date	Spot Market	Forward Market		
		1 month	3 months	6 months
British pound sterling—				
9/29/72				
Bid	2.4205	2.4148	2.4040	2.3879
Offer	2.4210	2.4159	2.4050	2.3892
Spread	.0005	.0011	.0010	.0013
British pound sterling—				
10/1/74				
Bid	2.3360	2.3320	2.3194	2.2983
Offer	2.3368	2.3332	2.3207	2.2996
Spread	.0008	.0012	.0013	.0013
Japanese yen—9/29/72				
Bid	.003321⅜	.003338⅜ [a]	.003381⅛	.003473⅜
Offer	.003322½	.003344½	.003393½	.003491½
Spread	.000001⅛	.000006⅛	.000012⅜	.000018⅛
Japanese yen—10/1/74				
Bid	.003352	.003350	.003337	.003335
Offer	.003355	.003357	.003346	.003344
Spread	.000003	.000007	.000009	.000009
German mark—9/29/72				
Bid	.3121⅝	.3130⅞	.3149⅜	.3174⅛
Offer	.3122⅛	.3132⅜	.3150⅝	.3176⅛
Spread	.0000½	.0001½	.0001¼	.0002
German mark—10/1/74				
Bid	.3774	.3779	.3796	.3808
Offer	.3778	.3785	.3803	.3816
Spread	.0004	.0006	.0007	.0008
Dutch guilder—9/29/72				
Bid	.3088½	.3098¼	.3117¾	.3139¼
Offer	.3089⅛	.3099⅞	.3119⅜	.3141⅞
Spread	.0000⅝	.0001⅝	.0001⅝	.0002⅝
Dutch guilder—10/1/74				
Bid	.3704½	.3708½	.3724½	.3736½
Offer	.3707½	.3713½	.3729½	.3741½
Spread	.0003	.0005	.0005	.0005

Table continues on following page

TABLE A-1 (continued)

Currency and Date	Spot Market	Forward Market		
		1 month	3 months	6 months
Swiss franc—9/29/72				
Bid	.2630	.2638½	.2655	.2676½
Offer	.2630⅝	.2639⅞	.2656⅛	.2678⅛ [b]
Spread	.0000⅝	.0001⅜	.0001⅛	.0001⅝
Swiss franc—10/1/74				
Bid	.3395	.3401½	.3406	.3416
Offer	.3398	.3406	.3410	.3423
Spread	.0003	.0004½	.0004	.0007
Canadian dollar—9/29/72				
Bid	1.0164½	1.0165½	1.0167½	1.0168
Offer	1.0167	1.0170	1.0172	1.0172½
Spread	.0002½	.0004½	.0004½	.0004½
Canadian dollar—10/1/74				
Bid	1.0151	1.0152	1.0162	1.0165
Offer	1.0154	1.0159	1.0168	1.0171
Spread	.0003	.0007	.0006	.0006
Italian lira—9/29/72				
Bid	.001718⅛	.001714⅝	.001709⅛	.001701⅛
Offer	.001718¾	.001717¼	.001711¾	.001703¾
Spread	.000000⅝	.000002⅝	.000002⅝	.000002⅝
Italian lira—10/1/74				
Bid	.001514	.001506	.001486	.001450
Offer	.001515	.001509	.001489	.001455
Spread	.000001	.000003	.000003	.000005
French franc–9/29/72				
Bid	.1994⅞	.1995⅜	.1998⅛	.2000⅝
Offer	.1995½	.1996⅝	.1999½	.2002¼
Spread	.0000⅝	.0001¼	.0001⅜	.0001⅝
French franc–10/1/74				
Bid	.2113	.2103	.2085	.2053
Offer	.2114	.2105	.2088	.2057
Spread	.0001	.0002	.0003	.0004

[a] In McKinnon's paper, the figure reported is .003378⅜, but that figure would appear to be in error.

[b] In McKinnon's paper, the figure reported is .2648⅛, but that figure would appear to be in error.

NOTE: Bid-asked price quotations and spreads for twelve-month forward rates have been omitted because of large incongruities in the rounding of data on bid and offer price quotations in McKinnon's paper; and bid-asked price quotations likely to be so affected, inasmuch as exchange rates are likely to be less variable over the long run. As a result, speculators' costs of holding open positions are likely to be reduced, thus permitting a smaller gap between the expected future spot rate and the current forward or futures rate.

The lower cost of distant-term hedging under floating rates is not apparent, however, because the cost is still prohibitive (no such hedging has taken place under either type of exchange rate system). Hedging of foreign exchange risk is usually of near-term maturities. In the opinion of Dennis Weatherstone, vice chairman of the board, Morgan Guaranty Trust Company, however, the switch to floating rates has generated a lengthening of maturities of forward contracts in the foreign exchange market.

For hedging that exists under both types of exchange rate system, we would expect the more distant-term transactions to be relatively less expensive under floating rates than under fixed rates, and nearer-term ones to be relatively more expensive. Economists, in comparing transaction costs under the two systems, have noted that transaction costs (as represented by bid-asked spreads) have been greater during the current floating rate system than during the previous fixed rate system.[4] Undoubtedly, part of the explanation is that the *ceteris paribus* assumption does not apply; instability in underlying economic conditions has been greater during the floating rate period than it was during the fixed rate period (taken as a whole). However, in the comments I have seen, the bid-asked spreads examined have been for forward contracts with a maturity of a year or less. Because all such contracts may be classified as "near-term" ones, the findings are not surprising. It is important, however, to place appropriate qualifications on those findings so that they do not mistakenly lead to incorrect assessments of the desirability of floating rates.

Ronald McKinnon has collected some valuable data on interbank bid-asked spreads in spot and forward markets from 1972 through

and spreads for the Belgian franc have been omitted because of the absence of quotations on this currency on October 1, 1974.

Source: Ronald McKinnon, "Floating Foreign Exchange Rates 1973-74: The Emperor's New Clothes," in Karl Brunner and Alan Meltzer, eds., *Institutional Arrangements and the Inflation Problem,* Carnegie-Rochester Series on Public Policy, vol. 3; published as Supplement 3 (1977) of *The Journal of Monetary Economics,* pp. 79-114.

[4] In particular, see Ronald McKinnon, "Floating Foreign Exchange Rates 1973-74: The Emperor's New Clothes," in Karl Brunner and Alan Meltzer, eds., *Institutional Arrangements and the Inflation Problem,* Carnegie-Rochester Series on Public Policy, vol. 3; published as Supplement 3 (1977) of the *Journal of Monetary Economics,* pp. 79-114.

1974.[5] The data on forward contracts relate to maturities of one year or less. Most of the spreads increased during this period. (The interbank spreads are part of the spreads facing hedgers and speculators.)

McKinnon notes that the spreads on forward contracts increased more than those on spot contracts and that the spreads on the longer-term forward contracts increased more than those on the nearer-term ones. The data in his paper, however, do not appear to support such conclusions. Table A-1 shows bid-asked price quotations and spreads in the interbank foreign exchange market for the earliest and the latest dates for which data were collected by McKinnon—September 29, 1972 (during the adjustable peg system of fixed rates) and October 1, 1974 (during the floating rate system).

It is true that the absolute change in spreads was in general larger for the longer-term forward contracts than for the nearer-term contracts, including the spot ones—although this did not occur for the British pound sterling or the Japanese yen. However, in those cases in which the spreads on the more distant-term contracts increased more than those on the nearer-term contracts (including the spot ones), they usually did so only in an arithmetic sense, not in a relative sense; this latter point seems to me the most relevant for this discussion. Indeed, in addition to the pound sterling and the Japanese yen, this was in general the case for the German mark, the Dutch guilder, and the Swiss franc. For two currencies—the Canadian dollar and the Italian lira—the results were inconclusive. Only for the French franc was the relative increase in spreads greater for the more distant-term contracts than for the nearer-term contracts, and even here the difference was not pronounced. With data on more distant-term forward contracts than those considered here, the findings on the change in relative costs of effecting transactions probably would be even more conclusive.

Governmental Policies under Floating Rates

The nature of governmental policy response to exchange rate problems is a crucial issue affecting the comparative advantage of floating rates in reducing distant-term risk and the cost of hedging such risk. Policy officials are deeply concerned about the international value of their country's currency. If there is a precipitous fall in its international value, they try to determine the contributory factor(s); if they discover the reason(s), which should not be a difficult task, they might take corrective measures.

---

[5] Ibid., "Floating Foreign Exchange Rates."

Unfortunately, however, policy officials might react initially to reductions in the international value of their currency in a different way. They might seek to use some or all of the paraphernalia—the ad hoc measures—that they used during the crisis periods of the Bretton Woods regime. This development could have serious consequences for a system of floating rates. The system of ad hoc measures typically expands, with ever-increasing adverse effects. Eventually, direct regulation of multinational activity might be imposed. Although the regulations might be directed at alleged speculation of multinationals, they would inevitably impair multinationals' ability to hedge their operations.[6]

This writer in fact expects policy officials initially to follow the route of the ad hoc measures, as happened with the June 1976 credit to Great Britain, as well as the massive, costly purchases and sales of foreign currencies. Inevitably, such measures will prove to be useless, unless they are accompanied by a more responsible governmental policy (in which case the measures would be unnecessary, except for a possible short-run effect or for a perverse desire to be subjected to control by other countries).[7] Only when this is accepted will there be any hope for a reasonably free market in foreign exchange, with all the attendant benefits that such a market would provide.

Because of the initial policy reactions to exchange rate problems, the initial benefits of the current system of floating rates are not likely to be as large as they ultimately will become. Furthermore, because of a recent pronouncement by the Financial Accounting Standards Board (Statement No. 8), a bias has been introduced against the system of floating rates.[8]

Conclusion

The switch to floating rates appears to generate a reduction in the distant-term foreign exchange risk to firms, with an increase in their near-term risk in certain situations and a decrease in others. The effect of the switch on their cost of hedging distant-term and near-term risk is likely to be of the same nature. For these reasons, floating rates would appear to favor long-term international investment, whereas fixed rates would appear to favor (perhaps only in a comparative-

---

[6] See Burns, *Accounting Standards.*

[7] The ad hoc measures can have a desirable short-run effect if they give a country time in which to work out more responsible economic policies.

[8] See Burns, *Accounting Standards.*

advantage sense) international commercial interests. In addition, the difference in comparative advantage is likely to become more pronounced, the longer the system of floating rates exists.

The important (and perhaps excessive) economic and political position of commercial interests (especially commercial banks, acting directly as well as through their central banks) in the leading industrial countries, as well as the customary (but unwarranted) suspicion of international investors and speculators, may help to explain why the adjustable peg system of fixed rates persisted for so long.

Paradoxically, in the long run, even commercial interests may be favored by floating rates. The increased rate of economic growth and development throughout the world, which would result from the higher rate of investment under floating rates, would induce a greater volume of international commercial business. Stated differently, the fixed rate system, through its neglect of long-term international investment, might well lead eventually to a smaller volume of international commerce than would occur under floating rates.

APPENDIX B

Tax Straddles in Futures

A straddle in futures often consists of a long position on one (or more) futures contracts on a given asset (say, March 1979 copper) and a short position on one (or more) futures contracts on the same asset, but of a different maturity (say, July 1979 copper). Until recently, individuals who realized substantial short-term capital gains in a given year could reduce and postpone their tax liabilities by using "tax straddles" in futures. The purpose was to offset the short-term capital gain by effecting a short-term capital loss on one leg of a straddle; the gain from the other leg of the straddle would count as capital income in the subsequent year.

Tax straddles could be entered into at any time during the year, but usually they would be placed in July and August. At or near December 31 of a given year, the losing position of the straddle would be closed out, and a new position immediately put in its place. This loss would be used to offset a capital gain during the year. After six months had elapsed from the time of the original straddle position—say, in January and February of the following year—the old position on one leg (with its gain) and the new position on the other leg (with a probable small gain or loss) would be closed out. The gain on the old position would be taxed as a capital gain in the new year.

The use of straddles in futures to reduce and postpone taxes has been widespread. Tax straddles in silver futures were the most common type, but straddles in gold and copper were also used.[1] There

---

[1] At times, straddles in silver have apparently accounted for more than 75 percent of open interest in silver futures. See "IRS Ruling on Silver Puts 'Butterfly Spread' Tax Shelter in Question," *Wall Street Journal*, June 6, 1978.

In all likelihood, the use of tax straddles in silver explains the unusually high ratio of open interest to transactions in silver futures; the holding of positions in futures for such purposes does not entail as much turnover of contracts (on balance) as that for other purposes.

were two principal reasons for the popularity of silver straddles: silver prices are subject to large fluctuations, and the price relationship between the different maturity dates of silver contracts usually has been reasonably stable.[2] Large price movements are needed to bring about gains on one leg of a straddle and losses on the other, whereas a reasonably stable price relationship of the different maturities helps to equalize the gain and the loss on the two legs of a straddle.

In two recent rulings, the Internal Revenue Service (IRS) has sought to eliminate the use of straddles in futures markets for the purpose of reducing and postponing taxes. The first ruling, 77–185 (issued on May 23, 1977), dealt with tax straddles in silver; the second, 78–414 (issued on November 20, 1978), with tax straddles in Treasury bills. The second ruling was prompted by developments arising out of the first.

IRS regulations allow deduction of capital losses (up to a limit) if such losses are sustained in closed and completed transactions, which were entered into for profit. In its 77–185 ruling, the IRS stated that the taxpayer's straddle transactions were not entered into for profit and that they were not "closed and completed" until the entire straddle position was lifted (in the following year).

Treasury bill futures had been regarded as a possible exception to this ruling, which dealt with commodity futures. Because gains on Treasury bills have been treated for tax purposes as ordinary income, Treasury bill futures were viewed by some as producing ordinary income gains and losses rather than capital gains and losses. Ordinary losses are deductible without limit up to the level of ordinary income, whereas capital losses are constrained by stricter guidelines. Straddles in Treasury futures, then, were regarded by some people as superior to those in silver as a form of tax shelter.

The crucial issue was whether Treasury bill futures were to be treated, for tax purposes, like Treasury bills or like futures contracts. The tax treatment of Treasury bills as income is probably based on the idea that an individual who purchases a bill at a discount and then sells it at or prior to maturity for a higher price has not incurred a risk of capital. Futures contracts, however, are treated as capital assets, so that gains or losses realized in the holding of these assets are treated as capital gains or losses.

---

[2] The large fluctuations of silver prices are attributable in part to changes in industrial and speculative demand; the reasonably stable price relationship of the different contract maturities, to the expected carry-over of large amounts of silver from one contract month to another. Recently, warehouse stocks of silver have fallen. This likely will work against the stable price relationship of the different contract maturities.

In a recent ruling, 78–414, the IRS sought to eliminate the use of straddles in Treasury bill futures for tax shelter purposes. In particular, it ruled that a Treasury bill futures contract is a capital asset and that any gains or losses on such a contract are to be treated as capital gains or losses.

Both the earlier IRS ruling (77–185) and the more recent one (78–414) view straddles as lacking economic risk, and therefore as being artificial tax minimization transactions. Such a view is of questionable validity inasmuch as straddles are often used by commercial firms for hedging purposes. Furthermore, straddles—whether for commercial use or as a tax shelter—entail an element of risk from the possible change in the price relationship of the different maturities.[3]

The first IRS ruling dealing with tax straddles has already been appealed to federal tax court, and the second one is likely to be. It is not at all clear how the courts will rule on the issues. The practical problem appears to be that of distinguishing appropriate from inappropriate uses of straddles in futures.

Even if the IRS rulings are upheld in court, straddles in Treasury bill futures are still likely to be used for tax purposes. However, such use is likely to entail greater risk. In particular, an individual who takes such a straddle will now have to hope that the gain occurs on the short leg of the straddle and that the loss occurs on the long side. If a loss does occur on the long side, an individual would opt for delivery and thereby be in a position to take an ordinary income loss.

Tax straddles in Treasury bill futures may present a problem to this futures market if deliveries on long positions were to become a sizable proportion of deliverable supplies. There is no evidence at present that such a problem has occurred. And, in view of the increased risk inherent in such straddles, their use is not likely to be of sufficient magnitude to present such a problem.

---

[3] It is, however, true that a so-called butterfly spread—entailing one (or more) long position(s) in a near-term futures contract and one (or more) in a distant-term contract and two (or more) short positions in an intermediate-term contract (or vice versa) may greatly reduce the risk of changes in the price relationship of the different maturities. And such spreads are used for tax purposes.

The *Wall Street Journal* states, "No one seems to know who first coined the name [butterfly spread], just that when diagramed a certain way the operation resembles a butterfly with wings spread open." "IRS Ruling."

APPENDIX C

Proposed Futures Contract on
Broad-Based Equity Security

In late 1977, the Kansas City Board of Trade proposed a futures contract on the Dow Jones Industrial Average. After a public hearing on that proposal in late 1978, the exchange revised its proposal—to a futures contract on the Standard and Poor's Composite Index of 500 stocks. This note is concerned with some economic aspects of a futures contract on a broad-based equity security. It first examines some economic benefits of such a futures contract. Then, it discusses some advantages of the exchange's revised proposal in comparison to its original one. Next, it examines a regulatory problem involving a futures contract on a broad-based equity security. Finally, it discusses the possible nondelivery aspect of futures contracts on a broad-based equity security.

Economic Benefits

A futures contract on a broad-based equity security is likely to provide two types of economic benefits: benefits to the direct users of the new instrument and—of likely greater significance—indirect benefits from the information the new instrument generates. The benefits would occur if the market were functioning properly and effective regulation were in place.

Direct Benefits. Today, there are many ways in which individuals and firms may hedge equity investments; for example, they may diversify security investments (including timely purchases and sales of debt securities) or sell call options on equity securities. The ability to hedge investments in equity securities through offsetting positions in a futures contract on a broad-based equity security would appear to enhance efficiency in hedging equity investments. In particular, the value of broad-based equity security futures would likely have a high correlation with the values of a wide array of equity securities, thus fostering large benefits from hedging; transactions and carrying costs of such hedging are likely to be small, at least for the near-term futures.[1]

Many types of investors are likely to use a futures contract on a broad-based equity security for hedging purposes. Institutional investors, with their large, diversified portfolios, could use such an instrument when they have bearish expectations or simply a large degree of uncertainty about the direction of stock prices; the use of this instrument would likely lower the transaction costs of moving in and out of a wide set of equity securities.

In addition, both institutional and individual investors would be likely to use such an instrument when they expect a limited number of securities (perhaps only one) to do either better or worse than the market as a whole. And such investors could use broad-based equity security futures no matter what their expectations are about the market as a whole—whether favorable, unfavorable, highly uncertain, or some combination thereof. This aspect of hedging involves offsetting one type of risk (the macro performance of equities) so as to bear more easily another type of risk (the micro, or relative, performance of specific equities).

For all security investors, the ability to hedge equity investments (taken as a whole) more efficiently would improve the risk-return trade-off in equity investments. As a result, they should become more willing to make equity investments, and their overall investment position would be strengthened.

Investment bankers who market new security issues may also use a futures contract on a broad-based equity security for hedging purposes. In particular, such a contract could reduce their risk of price uncertainty during the period of distribution. The demand for such a contract is most likely to occur when the price of a specific issue is expected to be well correlated with that of the broad-based issue. This type of hedging reduces the marketing costs of new security

---

[1] The low cost of carrying a position in a near-term equity security futures contract would be occasioned by low margin requirements, absence of default risk, together with a small difference that is likely to exist between a current futures price of a broad-based equity security and the spot price of such a security that is expected to exist in the future. The closeness of these two prices would be based on the willingness of speculative investors to take open positions in such futures on the side opposite to that of the preponderance of hedgers. See Chapter 3 of this study.

issues, thereby increasing the volume of such issues and fostering the liquidity of the market for existing securities.

Finally, dealers in existing securities, such as specialists, may use a broad-based equity security futures contract to reduce their costs of inventory holdings. Having the ability to hedge inventory holdings is likely to increase the volume of such holdings and to reduce bid-asked price spreads in existing security issues, and thus to increase the liquidity of such markets.

To be sure, some investors may switch their investments from securities to futures. Such substitution would reduce participation in securities markets. This effect would have to be balanced against the positive effects of broad-based equity security futures on participation in securities markets. The net effect on participation in securities markets is an empirical issue.

It is this writer's view that the favorable effects—indirect as well as direct—of a broad-based equity security futures contract are likely to outweigh the substitution effect. The important effect is that on the liquidity (and, more broadly, on the efficiency) of securities markets. The volume of investors' participation in securities markets is, of course, a relevant factor, but there are others such as the effects on investment bankers and securities dealers, and the important indirect effects.

Indirect Benefits. The development of a futures market for a broad-based equity security is likely to have some important indirect effects. First of all, it is likely to improve expectations about the future spot price of such an equity security. This information would facilitate the decision making of firms that issue, market, deal, and invest in equity securities, especially those with prices highly correlated with that of a broad-based equity security. In particular, such information may be of value in reaching financing decisions, including those on the volume and timing of security issues (equity and debt).

Secondly, the development of this futures market would convey useful information to and foster the working of related markets, such as those for equity securities, debt securities, and foreign currencies. Information flowing to equity markets (in general) would be improved, so equity prices (in general) would reflect more promptly changes that occur in expected demand-supply conditions.[2] The result-

---

[2] It is not clear whether short-run price changes of equity securities would be higher or lower. To be sure, the improved information flowing to markets for equity securities would tend to enhance such changes. However, the new hedging instrument likely would reduce the movement in and out of equity securities, and this would tend to dampen short-run fluctuations of prices.

ing faster economic adjustments by commercial firms would tend to generate smaller long-run changes in equity prices than would otherwise occur. This would reduce distant-term uncertainty about equity prices and increase investors' confidence in equity securities. The result could well be higher equity prices, a greater volume of equity issues, better debt-equity ratios, enhanced capital formation, a greater inflow of foreign capital (both to the equity and debt security markets), and a stronger international value of the dollar.

Advantages of Revised Proposal

The Dow Jones Industrial Average is probably the best known index, but it does not appear to be the optimal one from the standpoint of a futures contract based on a general stock index. The Standard and Poor's Composite Index of 500 stocks appears to be a superior index of an average stock portfolio, and thus a futures contract on it might be used to a greater extent for hedging purposes.

In particular, the Standard and Poor's Index is more representative of the market as a whole than is the Dow Jones Index; it encompasses a larger and more representative group of securities than the Dow, and it takes into account the volume of outstanding issues as well as price, whereas the Dow takes into account only the price of a security. The Dow is marred not only by its underrepresentation of the whole market, but also by continual changes in the nature of its representation as new securities are issued and stock splits occur. The narrowness of the Dow Jones Industrial Average might, however, be an advantage if delivery were to be included in the futures contract's terms and conditions.

A futures contract on the Standard and Poor's Composite Index would probably be less subject to price manipulation than the Dow. With equal quantity weights given to all securities in the Dow, those whose issues were relatively thin in volume and high in price might be subjected to manipulative pressures.

Practical Problem

There is a difficult jurisdictional issue involving the regulation of broad-based equity security futures. In particular, the issue is whether CFTC regulation of this market would be compatible with Federal Reserve and SEC regulation of securities markets.

Margin requirements for spot securities and short positions in securities and mutual funds are regulated by the Federal Reserve and the SEC, respectively. These regulations have been promulgated after careful study of the issues involved. When it is remembered that as a futures contract approaches maturity, it more and more resembles a spot contract, Federal Reserve and SEC concerns in this area would appear to warrant careful attention.

Because any malfunctioning in a spot, futures, or option market is likely to have adverse spillover effects on the others, the orderly functioning of any new market in our current environment is imperative. For this reason, agency cooperation in the surveillance of the related markets and in investigations of possible market problems would appear to be essential.[3] In view of SEC concerns about security options, a deliberative approach to a proposed broad-based equity security futures would appear to be warranted.

Delivery Provisions

There has been a lot of discussion about the possible nondelivery aspect of futures contracts on broad-based equity securities. This aspect does not appear to be an economic problem. Contracts for future transactions have developed gradually from tailor-made forward contracts in which deliveries were almost always effected to standardized futures contracts in which deliveries are seldom carried out (and this is true whether or not speculative investors are considered). A deliveryless futures contract for a broad-based equity security may be viewed as the culmination of this historical development.

This does not mean that a deliveryless futures contract would be desirable for all assets. The delivery feature serves at least two purposes. First, it introduces a certain discipline into the setting of terms and conditions of a contract. In particular, it is likely to encourage consistency between the terms and conditions of a futures contract and commercial practices in the spot market. Second, it provides an unambiguous means of settling contracts.

Each of these purposes is useful. However, for some futures contracts, delivery may not be needed to achieve these purposes. A futures contract on a broad-based equity security would not seem to require the discipline of retaining commercial usefulness of contracts. A weighted average of a broad-based stock index is self-adjusting in terms of commercial usefulness. In addition, for futures

---

[3] Such cooperation would be essential whether or not a broad-based equity futures includes a delivery provision. To be sure, if the contract's terms were to include a delivery provision, the SEC's role probably would be greater.

on such an index, there would be little ambiguity about the price at settlement, inasmuch as the index is based on liquid assets for which prices are widely known with a high degree of precision.

The above points suggest considerations that may be of use to the commission in judging whether a delivery provision is desirable: Is delivery important in retaining commercial usefulness of a contract? Is delivery important in securing an unambiguous means of settlement? These questions apply to any futures contracts, existing or proposed. It would appear that delivery provisions would be useful for futures on most commodities but would be of little value for futures on broad-based equity securities.

INDEX

transactions in spot markets 75; and planning and pricing decisions 76; and efficiency of related markets 76; and bid-asked price spreads in spot markets 77; and regional differences in spot prices 77-78; and spot price variability 78-79; and competition 79; and prices and commercial practices in forward markets 80-81; some recent innovations in 81-82; and non-market arena 82-83; government regulation of 92-100; and governmental policies 111-14; and public criticism 101, 115-17

Futures prices, premiums embedded in. *See* Hedging; Speculation

Futures Trading Act of 1978, 101, 106, 107

Galbraith, John Kenneth 116

Garbade, Kenneth D., on improvements in communication 16n.; on stock options 65n.

Ghana 94

Gold, and market development 23; and indexed contracts 48n.; tax straddles 127

Goss, B. A., on price trends 11n.; on speculation 21n.-22n.; on origin of forward markets 41n.; on normal backwardation 44n.; on futures markets and price variability 79n.; on controversial nature of futures markets 101n.

Government National Mortgage Association Securities, bid-asked spreads and GNMA futures 77, 106; regional differences in rates and GNMA futures 77-78; standardization of and GNMA futures 81; contract designation of GNMA futures 103-4

Governmental nonregulatory policies 10, 24-25, 29, 48, 60, 80, 81, 96, 115-16; nature of governmental deliberations 111; price stabilization efforts 112; fiscal and monetary policy 113-14; short-run bias of 113, 115-16; floating exchange rates 114, 124-26

Governmental regulatory policies 10, 24-25, 29, 81; benefits 89-90; costs 90-91; securities 91; futures 92-100; commodity options 100-2

Grading, of commodities 14, 29. *See also* Standardization

Grain elevator, and hedging 36

Gray, Roger W. 49n.; on speculation 21n.-22n.; on origin of forward contracts 40n.

Great Britain 125

Great Depression 115

Gurley, John G. 12n.

Hedging 34, 96; example of 36; benefits of 37-38, 86; costs of 38-39, 75, 81, 83, 86, 93, 99, 103; and emergence of commercial demand for forward contracts 40-45; and risk transfer 46; selective 47; forward versus futures contracts 54; and emergence of commercial demand for options 58; options on actuals versus options on futures 65; options versus futures 65-66; and foreign exchange risk 120-24; and equity investments 131-33

Hedging, cross, 54-55

Hicks, J. R., on fixprice markets 43n.; on normal backwardation 43n., 44n.; on interest rates 48; on market development and gaps in prices 87n.

Homogeneity. *See* Standardization

Houthakker, Hendrick S., on normal backwardation 44n.

Incorporation, and market information 15; and risk reduction 37

Indexed contracts, and price uncertainty 48

Inflation, and storage costs 23; improved information on 81-82, 85-86, 115-16; and governmental policies 112-13; and price uncertainty 113

Information, element of a market 5-6; and standardization 14, 19, 32, 50; and brand-name investments 15; and incorporation 15; and financial rating services 15-16; and financial intermediation 16; and market news reports 16; and improvements in communication 16; and related assets 16-17; and insurance 18; and definition and enforcement of property rights 18-19; spot transactions versus forward contracts 19; and improvements in transportation 20; and inventory holding 20-23; and speculation 21-22, 40-42, 45, 47-48; and orderly market conditions 24-25, 28-29; and market organization 29, 52-53, 64-65; and efficiency of futures markets 33-34; and emergence of futures markets 35; and commercial demand for forward contracts 37-38; forward contracts versus futures contracts 54; and emergence of option contracts 58; and emergence of option markets 62; important indirect benefits of improving market efficiency 70-74, 75-82, 83-87; and governmental regulatory policies 89-91; and governmental nonregulatory policies 111-14

Inside information, securities markets 27-28; of governments 82, 112; in futures trading 94-97

Insurance costs, and default risk 18; fire or theft 23; and property rights 23; and arbitrage costs 43; reductions of 74

Internal Revenue Service, on tax straddles 128-29

International investment. *See* Multinational companies; Capital investment

International Tin Agreement 112

International trade, and fixed and floating exchange rates 112, 125-26, 117

Inventories, and market liquidity 20-24; and demand for forward and futures contracts 35-37, 40, 42-43; and demand for option purchases 58, 59; and writing of options 63; and benefits of market development 71, 73, 75, 76, 79, 81, 83, 84-86, 132-33

Irwin, H. S. 40n.; on forward markets 50n., 51n.; on futures markets 52n.

Jarecki, Henry 59n.-60n.
Journal of Commerce 61n.

Kaicher, Monica M., on stock options 65n.

Kalecki, M., on risk 46n.

Kansas City Board of Trade, and spot price quotations 107-8; and futures for equity security 131

Keynes, John Maynard 40n.; on price trends 11n.; on role and cost of speculation 41; on normal backwardation 42; and *The General Theory* 115

Klein, Benjamin, on price uncertainty 113n.

Lang, Richard W. 82n.
Lavington, Frederick 12n., 72n.
Liquidity, *See* Market liquidity
Liquidity proper, defined 8. *See also* Price uncertainty

London exchanges, options on futures 57; marketability of options 63; and fraudulent option sales 100

Margin requirements, and market liquidity 25, 51-52; and opportunity costs 39, 41, 53; reducing default cost 50-51; and clearinghouses 52; and trend trading 53n.; and exchanges 54; and daily price limitations 99-100; and government regulation 134-35

Marketability, meaning of term 8; relationship with price uncertainty 9, 49. *See also* Liquidity

Market conditions, meaning of orderly and disorderly 9-12; and monopolies 24-25, 28; and rumors 25; and destabilizing trading activity 25; and contract specification 53; and governmental policies 81, 89-91, 92-97, 99, 100-1, 102, 103, 105, 106, 111, 112

Market efficiency, meaning of term 7-12, 33-35, 63; and market liquidity 13-24; and market conditions 24-25; and market organization 25-28, 29, 50-55, 62-65; role of market participants 35-49, 57-62; benefits of improving 69-88; and market regulation 89-102; and governmental policies 111-14, 119-26

Market development, defined 6-7. *See also* Market efficiency

Market liquidity, defined 8-9; and market conditions, market organization 7-8, 10-12, 24-25, 28-29; breadth and urgency of demand 13, 39-42, 45, 58-59; quality evaluation costs 13-17, 53, 64; default costs 17-19, 50-51, 64; transportation costs 19-20; carrying costs 20-24, 53-54; and transaction costs 63, 64, 70, 74, 75, 83; and decision making 71, 74, 76, 83; and related markets 71-72, 76-79, 80-81, 83-87; and market integration 72-73; as inducement to innovations 73-74; recent innovations 81-83; and market regulation 89-91; and governmental policies 111-15. *See also* Hedging; Speculation

Market news reports, and market liquidity 16, 20, 111

Market organization, meaning of term 12; application of economies of scale 25-26, 51, 62; and agricultural products 26-28; brokers, futures commission merchants 29, 99-100; exchanges

141

29, 53-54, 64-65, 97-99; margin requirements 50-51, 53; standardization 50, 53; clearinghouses 51-52; dealers 63; and commodity options 100-2; and regulatory approval 116

Market regulation. *See* Governmental regulatory policies

Market surveillance, in futures 93-94, 107; agency cooperation in 135

Markets, defined 5. *See also* Spot markets; Forward markets; Futures markets; Option markets

Markets, cash, defined 78; and futures markets 78

Markets, centralization of, and transportation costs 19-20; some historical aspects of 26-27; and forward contracts 50; and futures 53; and market development 74

Markets, decentralization of, some historical aspects of 27; and market development 78-79

Markets for future transactions, defined 31. *See also* Forward markets; Futures markets; Option markets

Markets, integration of, and centralization 19-20, 27; and quality price differences 72-73; and price variability 73; and competition 73; and regional price differences 77; and risk assessments 84-87

Markets, integrity of, and inside information 96-97; and dual trading 98; and customers' funds 99; and daily price limitations 99; and the Commodity Futures Trading Commission 100; and fraudulent sales of options 100. *See also* Inside information; Monopolies

Markets, orderly functioning of, defined 7-8; and government regulation 89-91

Markets, optimal benefits of, defined 8; and government regulation 89, 92

Markets, perfect, meaning of term 70, 78; and market development 70, 78

Markets, thin, confusion with illiquidity 9; suggestions for special regulatory attention 90

Markets, to arrive, defined 78; and futures markets 78

Marshall, Alfred 40n.; on market liquidity 13n.; on price fluctuations 36n.; on perfect markets 70, 78; on consumers' surplus 71n.; on option

markets 102; the theory of countervailing power 116

McKinnon, Ronald, on bid-asked spreads in foreign exchange markets 121-24

Mill, John Stuart, on speculation 21n.-22n.

Minneapolis Grain Exchange, and spot price quotations 107-8

Monetary policy, and inflation 113; and emphasis on money supply 114; and futures on debt securities 115-16; and futures on foreign exchange 116

Money, development of 6

Monopolies, and disorderly conditions 10, 24; in foreign exchange market 28; temporary 93-94; structural 94-97. *See also* Competition

Moody's, and market information 15

Moral risk 17-19

Multinational companies, and foreign exchange risk 81; and governmental policy 96, 125-26. *See also* Capital investment; Foreign exchange

New York City 25, 26, 109

New York Coffee and Sugar Exchange, and spot price quotations 107-8

Nonmarket transactions, and market development 74, 82-83

Normal backwardation. *See* Backwardation

Onion futures, prohibition of 79n., 103

Open interest, defined 32; growth of, in futures 33, 100; and illiquid markets 49; asymmetry between puts and calls 59; in stock options 64-65; of foreign governments in futures 95-97

Opportunity costs, defined 39; element of carrying cost of forward contracts 38-39, 41; element of carrying cost of option grantors 58; and lower interest rates 86

Option contracts, definition of puts and calls 57; raison d'être 58; premiums on 59-62, 83, 85; open interest of 59; and dealers 63; on equity securities 64-65; the choice among options 65

Option markets, Ch. 4; meaning of term 5-6, 57; efficiency of 7-12, 63; development of option contracts 57-62; and futures 62-63; dealers in 63; exchanges and standardization 64-65; and effects on price expectations 83-84; and effects on market efficiency 84; and effects on risk assessment

84-87; government regulation of 91, 100-2; and governmental policies 111-14; and public criticism 115-17

Option premiums, meaning of term 57-58, 60; and striking prices 59-61; and contract maturities 59-60; and governmental policy 60; implicit versus explicit 60-62; market organization and bid-asked spreads on 64; and market information 83-87

Options Clearing Corporation 64-65

Options, grantor of, meaning of term 57; costs 58-59; implicit payments to 60-62; dealers as 63; and exchanges 64

Options, striking price of, meaning of term 57; raison d'être 58; and option premiums 59, 60, 61, 62; and option dealers 63; exchange specification of 64; and information on 83, 85

Orderly market conditions. See Market conditions

Parks, Richard W., on relative price variability 48n., 113n.

Political risk 18

Poole, William, on interest rate expectations 82n.

Price controls 80; and market efficiency 112-13

Price level, and market development 70, 71, 75, 76. See also Inflation

Price spreads, bid-asked, in foreign exchange markets 121-24. See also Transaction costs

Price uncertainty, meaning of term 8; relationship with marketability 9, 49; macro versus micro 48; and contract maturities 49, 60, 123; and option premiums 58-59, 63, 85-87; near-term and distant-term 73, 79, 81, 84, 99n.-100n., 112-14, 119-26. See also Liquidity

Price uncertainty, exposure to, raison d'être 35-36; cost of, meaning of term 37; reduction of cost through hedging 37-38, 58; and backwardation 42-44; and asymmetry of puts and calls 59; and benefits of options 102. See also Inventories; Foreign exchange

Price variability, and speculation 21-22, 48; versus the basis 36, 37-38; of forward prices 48-49; and option contracts 59-60; near-term and distant-term 73, 79, 81, 84, 99n.-100n., 119-26; and governmental policies 112-14

Property rights, and enforcement costs 18-19; and insurance costs 23; improvements in system of 74; and governmental policies 111, 113

Puts. See Option contracts

Quality of assets, and market liquidity 13, 71, 74; standardization 14, 35, 50, 80-81; price uncertainty 15; brand-name investments 15; incorporation 15; financial rating services 15-16; financial intermediation 16; collection and dissemination of information 16-17; specification of contracts 31, 58; assets versus services 32; exchange specification of 53, 54, 64, 93; options and futures 62

Quality deterioration, costs of, and market development 23; and arbitrage between spot and forward prices 43-44

Quantity of assets, ease of ascertaining 13n.; specification of contracts 31, 57; exchange specification of 54, 64, 93; options and futures 62

Rainbolt II, John V. 104n.

Rasche, Robert H. 82n.

Raw materials 13, 40, 49, 77

Refrigeration, and market liquidity 23. See also Storage costs

Risk transfer 46-47, 66-67

Rumors, and barriers to information 10-11, 25; and futures 92

Rutledge, David J. S., on speculation 21n.-22n.; on origin of forward contracts 40n.

Ruttan, Vernon W. 73n.-74n.

Schmooker, Jacob 73n.-74n.

Schultz, Charles 73n.-74n.

Search costs, intensive and extensive 13. See also Transaction costs

Securities, distinguished from commodities 6; information on 14-15; and financial intermediation 16; and cost of transportation 19-20; and cost of holding inventories 22, 23; of New York City 25; and market organization 27; similarity of securities futures and commodity futures 33; futures for debt 49, 52, 81-82; precise specification of and options for 57; Alcoa 60-62; options on equity 63, 64-65; regulation of 91; futures for equity 103-6, 131-35; and tax straddles 128-29

Cover and book design: Pat Taylor